Grit and GRACE

HEROIC WOMEN OF THE BIBLE

Grit and GRACE

HEROIC WOMEN OF THE BIBLE

By Caryn Rivadeneira

Illustrations by Katy Betz

SPARK
HOUSE
FAMILY

First edition published 2017
Printed in the United States of America
23 22 21 20 19   3 4 5 6 7 8 9

ISBN: 9781506424958
Ebook ISBN: 9781506426914

Written by Caryn Rivadeneira
Illustrations by Katy Betz
Designed by Mighty Media

Library of Congress Cataloging-in-Publication Data
Names: Rivadeneira, Caryn Dahlstrand, author. | Betz, Katy, illustrator.
Title: Grit and grace : heroic women of the Bible / by Caryn Rivadeneira ;
    illustrations by Katy Betz.
Description: Minneapolis : Sparkhouse Family, 2017.
Identifiers: LCCN 2017008137 | ISBN 9781506424958 (pbk. : alk. paper)
Subjects: LCSH: Women in the Bible--Juvenile literature. | Women in the
    Bible--Biography. | Girls--Religious life--Juvenile literature.
Classification: LCC BS575 .R585 2017 | DDC 220.9/2082--dc23
LC record available at https://lccn.loc.gov/2017008137

V63474; 9781506424958; OCT2017

Sparkhouse Family
510 Marquette Avenue
Minneapolis, MN 55402
sparkhousefamily.org

To Greta

My girl

Who's been gritty and graceful
from the get-go

About the Author

Caryn Rivadeneira is the author of seven books. Caryn is a regular contributor to CT Women's blog and Aleteia's For Her. When not writing, you can find Caryn at church, where she works part-time, or hanging out with her husband, Rafael, their three kids, and their beloved rescued pit bull.

Contents

Foreword

When I received a copy of the book you hold in your hands now, one of my daughters picked it up to read. She's about your age, I think, and she's the eldest of four—she has two sisters and a brother. When her friends come over, these girls are just as likely to be reenacting epic Star Wars battle scenes as they are to be doing crafts. Her favorite books all feature heroes fighting evil, saving the world, defending the weak, leading the charge. Girls have a craving for a hero, too. Later that night, I went looking for the book and I found it in her room. She was sprawled on her bed, reading, unable to put it down.

We began to talk about the book and I asked her, so which one of these women is your favorite? Miriam? Mary? Esther?

She tipped her head thoughtfully and said, "Definitely the girl who put a tent peg through that guy's skull."

I burst out laughing. (That's Jael, by the way, and you'll meet her in the chapter about Deborah.) Not the usual Sunday School answer, is it?

It made me remember all those years ago when I was pregnant with her. I remember going to the bookstore to browse through all of the children's literature because I loved to read as a child and I couldn't wait to introduce my own children to these stories. I pictured us curled up on the couch, reading *Charlotte's Web* or *Anne of Green Gables* or *The Lion, The Witch, and the Wardrobe*. Books were such a big part of my life as a child—they still are, to be honest—and the characters all deeply shaped my thinking and my way of seeing the world.

But I began to see a pattern: most of the books geared toward boys were about heroes and adventures, while most of the books for girls were about princesses and tea parties and friendship dilemmas. Even when I went to look in the Christian section, I found so many books about the men of the Bible—David, Paul, Gideon, Joshua, Moses, Abraham—but hardly any books about the women of the Bible. I wondered, "What about the women? Where are the women who are heroes for my daughters to see? Where are the reminders to my son that women are heroes too?"

We can somehow get the idea that the women of the Bible were secondary characters or assistants, and so that women were not important or that they were incidental in God's story. We can even get the idea that to be a woman of God means to fit a small box of behavior or work or identity or expectation. We can pick up the idea from our culture that girls aren't valuable and that girls can't be heroes or leaders.

But instead, in the stories of the Bible, we see women of God who kicked every stereotype to the side and followed God with grit and with grace. In this book you're about to read, you'll meet women who were preachers, women who were prophets, women who were leaders, women who were pastors, evangelists, teachers, and army commanders! You will meet women who are brave and bold, women who were wily and clever, women who were fully alive, women who were flawed—just like us!—and yet said "yes!" to God.

You have a lineage of bold and unapologetic women behind you. You stand on the shoulders of these women even if you don't know it yet, women who loved God and loved people and showed up for their own lives with grit and with grace. You are more like them than you realize.

And you're a part of this big glorious story. You are! You're not a secondary character. And your story isn't for "someday"—someday when you're all grown up or when you finish school or if you get married or have children or whatever your "someday" has become in your dreaming.

Your story with God is already happening; you're in the midst of it. God's story doesn't start someday for you— you're an important part of the story already just as you are and just in this moment of your life.

That's why I was so happy to read Caryn's book! In these pages, you'll find some of the women who will mess with your idea of what it means to be a girl in God's story: Miriam, Rahab, Leah, Priscilla, Deborah. These stories will give you a picture of what it looks like to say "yes!" to God in your own time and in your own place. It will remind you that being a girl after God's own heart is an adventure and it is still the greatest story ever told.

—Sarah Bessey

Author of *Jesus Feminist* and *Out of Sorts: Making Peace with an Evolving Faith*

Introduction

When I was seven, my family attended a church with a bookstore inside it. I didn't love this church (the kids there weren't always very nice), but I did love the bookstore.

It had four pale yellow walls and a door, along with shelves full of books and Bibles and devotionals and quilted Bible covers and pens.

One week I spotted a basket on the floor. Inside were tiny little square books. I knelt down to see what these were and was greeted by names I didn't recognize: Hannah, Dorcas, Naomi.

These were stories about girls! Girls I hadn't heard of—and yet, girls (women, actually) whose stories were told in the Bible because they mattered. As I held the tiny books, thumbing the pages and studying the pictures, something stirred in me. I had to have these books! I needed to know their stories. I didn't know why they mattered, but something told me they did. That I'd discover things in these little books about these women that I didn't find in other Bible stories.

Though I loved the stories of the great men of the Bible (David and Samuel will always be my favorites), they were, well, men of the Bible. And I was a girl.

Not that I couldn't relate to or learn something from these men, but something about their stories kept me at arm's length from the Bible. They kept me from recognizing that God made women and girls to do amazing and mighty things just like God made men and boys to. As soon as I began to read these little books, I knew: I wanted to learn all about the women whose stories shaped the story of God and God's people—the Bible! And in learning about those women, I learned about all women: whom God loves and equips to do mighty things.

It's been a long time since I first read those little square books. But my curiosity about the women of the Bible has never died away. I've continued to read and learn about them throughout my whole life.

Which is what I hope *Grit and Grace* helps you do too. I hope not only that you can learn from their stories and their lives, but that as you re-imagine their stories with me, you might even see some of yourself in these stories. You might begin to imagine how your own life and your own story matters to God—and to this world.

The book is called *Grit and Grace* not only because the women of the Bible show grit (which means a tough, can-do spirit) and grace (which means a strong elegance or courageous kindness), but also because it's what I believe God made all of us to do. Living with grit and grace is one of the best ways to honor God as we go about our days—and as we learn about these women, their stories can inspire and motivate us to live out of our own grit and grace.

A few things about this book:

1. Though these stories are based on the Bible, this is not the Bible. I've imagined a lot of stuff here. I read the actual Bible stories, researched the women, prayed about how to tell you about them, and then let my imagination go to work. But just because we imagine something doesn't mean it's not—or can't be—true. Putting ourselves in the shoes of these women lets us imagine what it might look like to show both grit and grace as we live out our part of God's story.

2. The women of the Bible had very different lives than most of us know today—though, some women around the globe still live in similar ways. The women you'll read about here lived under a set of rules that don't make a lot of sense to us today, rules about what women should wear and talk about and do with their lives. It could be pretty scary to be a woman in Bible times. Many of the women you'll meet had to take huge risks to follow God, risks that meant breaking the rules about what was expected and accepted. To me, this is what makes their stories so powerful.

3. I've included stuff in each chapter to help you think about what you've read:

   Fast Facts: These tidbits give you a behind-the-scenes look at some of the issues these women faced and some insight into their lives.

   Think About It: These questions are there to reflect on the story you just read. You can also talk about them with a friend or over dinner with your family. Use them to help you consider how you can show grit and grace in your own life.

Get the Full Story: Every chapter is based on a real story from the Bible, so make sure to take a look at what the Bible writers said about these women. Some of them get only a sentence or two and some of them, a whole book!

Prayer Prompt: Every chapter ends with something for you to talk to God about. If you don't have a regular habit of praying right now, these can be an easy way to get started.

4. My favorite thing about the Bible is that God gave it to us to be wrestled with and wondered about. I don't believe for one moment that God lays out everything perfectly clearly in the Bible. Some things are really hard to believe or make sense of. So if you find yourself asking "What on earth?" or "How can that be?" or even if some stories make you wonder about God's goodness or faithfulness, that's okay. Take those questions to your parents or another adult you trust. Take them to your pastor. Take them to other places in the Bible. Take them to friends or books. Take them to God. God can handle anything—even our big, hard questions.

God will never love you less for asking questions. If these stories tell us anything, it's that God wants us to be curious and questioning, gritty and graceful.

—Caryn Rivadeneira

Chapter 1

Eve

I jumped at the loud "Caw-caw!" behind me. My head spun back. It was just Crow. *Why did his song suddenly send shivers up my spine?*

I turned back to the tree, wiped the juice from my chin, (*Why did this juice bother me so much?*) and swatted Fly, who buzzed around my piece of fruit. As my hand smacked him, he froze and fell to the ground.

What had I done?

I squatted to rouse Fly, but he wouldn't get up. He wouldn't fly.

Age: Unknown

Era: The beginning

"What's the matter with Fly?" I asked Serpent.

But as I stood to face him, Serpent thrust his tongue forward and hissed at me. I stepped back slowly.

Why hadn't I noticed the thick ripple of muscle as he wrapped himself through the gnarled limbs of the Tree of the Knowledge of Good and Evil? Why hadn't I ever before wondered if he would squeeze *me* like that?

I took another step back and readied myself to run, but then I remembered: *Adam!*

He'd taken his fruit around the other side of the thick, twisting tree. Adam crouched under the branches, devouring the fruit as though he'd never eaten, as though we hadn't spent our whole lives enjoying the ripest peaches and pears, the crunchiest carrots and cucumbers, the plumpest blueberries and raspberries. The way Adam tore at and sucked the fruit, you'd think we hadn't learned to pound corn and wheat into flour, adding fresh water from the stream and baking bread over sparking fires.

"Adam," I whispered, "we've got to get out of here."

As Adam looked around the trunk of the tree, I drew

my hands to my chest.

I was naked! How had I not realized this? I ran to the nearest fig tree and grabbed leaf after leaf, desperate to cover myself.

What was going on?

Adam stood up. I rushed behind the tree.

"Wait," I said. "Don't come any closer." And I threw fig leaves at him. "Cover yourself!"

I wasn't sure what was scarier—being naked in front of Adam or realizing the serpent was sliding his way down the trunk toward him.

"Never mind!" I yelled. "Run!"

Adam and I took off running, swatting gnats and mosquitoes, tossing aside limbs, and kicking past wildflowers that scratched our bare legs.

I motioned to a tangle of grapevines,

Fast Facts

◊ According to the Bible, Adam lived 930 years. No mention of how long Eve lived.

◊ *Eden* is thought to mean "fruitful, well-watered."

◊ The biblical account of creation is not at odds with the scientific accounts of creation. Both use the information the authors had at the time. Both pictures point to a Creator God.

◊ The Bible includes two back-to-back creation stories. The first, in Genesis 1, doesn't mention the "apple" incident at all. That shows up in the second creation story in Genesis 2 and 3. Eve doesn't get her name until the end of the story. Until then, she's just called "the woman."

and we dove into them, our shoulders heaving as we breathed deep and heavy. My chest tightened; water dripped down my face. Where once we had run through this garden, racing up its hills, splashing through its streams and ponds, climbing its trees without effort, now our muscles shook with exhaustion; our knees and ankles creaked under us.

As we hid, I pulled off vines and knotted them around the fig leaves I'd managed to carry with me. Somehow I created clothes to cover Adam. To cover me. To cover us.

But no matter how many vines we wrapped around our trembling bodies, no matter how deep we hid among the grapes that now rotted and dripped on the vine, we were exposed.

We'd done something awful. We'd disobeyed God. And now we were paying the price.

I've replayed the moment a million times in my head. It all happened so quickly. Or so I thought.

Serpent had asked me one question: "Did God *really* say you couldn't eat from all the trees in this garden?"

I laughed. "No. God said we could eat from *every* tree in the garden. Except—" I pointed to the tree just beyond us—"that one."

"And why not that one?" Serpent asked, as he slithered across the grass to the very tree.

"God said we'll die if we eat from it. If we *touch* it, even."

"Is that right?" Serpent asked as he slithered up the tree's trunk. "If you *touch* it?"

Get the Full Story
Genesis 1-4

And he hugged the tree's trunk tighter, reaching the tip of his tail toward a branch. Then toward a leaf. Then a piece of fruit.

"I'm not dead," Serpent said.

I took a step closer. Serpent did look fine.

"You want to know the *real* reason you can't eat the fruit?" Serpent asked.

I nodded.

"Because if you eat this fruit, you'll know as much as God. So go ahead," Serpent said. "Try it. You won't die. In fact, you'll be more alive than ever—your eyes will be wide open."

And so I reached forward and plucked a piece of fruit. I paused for a moment, wondering if I would drop dead. But I didn't. I closed my eyes and held the fruit to my nose. It smelled like a rose with a lemony twist.

I took a bite. And I did not die.

It was delicious! Better than anything I'd tasted. Adam, who'd been listening to my conversation with Serpent, stepped closer to me as I munched the fruit. I plucked another piece and handed it to him.

"You won't believe how good this is!" I said.

"But we're not supposed to," he said.

"Yeah, well, I didn't die," I said as Adam crunched into the fruit—again and again—grabbing another piece before diving behind the tree when Crow cawed.

The memory of what we'd done was interrupted by rustling. Adam and I turned toward it at the same time.

My heart sank.

In my terror running from Serpent, in my fear over what we'd done, I'd forgotten the One who'd walked through this garden with us, who created us, the One who'd given us a place of honor and responsibility in this perfect place, the One who'd been present as we'd played and named things and cooked and laughed and loved each other and the world around us. I'd forgotten God.

But God didn't forget us. We could hear the rustle of God moving closer.

"Keep still," Adam whispered.

I nodded.

The rustling stopped.

"Adam," God said.

Adam didn't answer. I held my breath.

"Adam, where are you?" God asked again.

This time, Adam scrambled from the bushes. I followed him. Slowly.

"I'm here, God," he said.

"Why were you hiding?" God asked.

"Because we were naked," Adam said. He grabbed my hand and helped me out from the bushes.

God looked at us with soft eyes and spoke with sadness. I adjusted my leaves.

"Who told you that you were naked?" God said. "Did you eat from the tree I told you not to eat from?"

Adam's eyes grew dark and he turned toward me, a long finger pointed my way.

"This woman," Adam hissed. "The one you put here with me—she gave me the fruit."

I stepped forward, toward God. Tears filled my eyes. I longed to feel God's warm nearness as I once had. Instead, I shivered.

"Serpent lied to me, and I ate it," I said.

Adam had blamed God and me. I blamed Serpent—and myself.

But God saw past the blame. God saw where each of us had failed. Though every wrong of the world would be placed on my shoulders, God saw it differently. Serpent had tricked us, but Adam and I? We had both disobeyed God. We had both forgotten who we were. We had *both* brought darkness and shame into the world. And we both paid the price.

The life I had known—a life without pain or heartache, a life where God and Adam and I lived in peace and wholeness—was over. God was hurt and angry. We had broken God's heart.

Now we would live outside the garden—away from the immediate, touchable presence of God—and now we *would* die.

But God, in God's great mercy, didn't leave us alone. God sent us out of the garden, but God's love, God's Spirit, and God's grace and goodness went with us.

We felt God with us in the clothes God made for us from animal skins.

We felt God with us in the laughter of our first sons, as they took first steps through our vegetable garden, as they learned to speak the names of the animals *we'd* named before everything changed.

We felt God with us as we told our sons the story of a good, good creation—of how Adam had been alone, how I was created, and how our togetherness, our partnership made the world *good*. We told them of how God had been so near, how we'd forgotten God, but how God had never forgotten us.

And we felt God with us on a day as dark as the day we were cast from the garden: the day my boy Cain killed my boy Abel. I never felt the curse more strongly. I had never felt such grief, such regret. It was my fault.

But I also remembered God's promise—in the middle

of the curse—that this was not the end. That Serpent had not won, and all was not lost. God promised that one day Serpent's power would be shut off—his head would be crushed!—by a Savior who would make the world perfect once again. One day Adam and I would walk, with our boys, through the garden we'd left—all of us alive, no longer fighting, or hating, or living under the curse.

God was good.

Think About It

Draw or write anything this story makes you think about.

How have you noticed God in nature?

How do you typically respond when someone blames you for something? How do you wish you responded?

Before they were thrown out of the garden, God gave Eve and Adam clothes. What does that tell you about God?

Prayer Prompt

What do you need to help you make good decisions? Wisdom maybe? Patience? Trust? Whatever it is, ask God to help you develop a bit more of this.

Chapter 2

Hagar

Call me Hagar.

    I am the mother of Ishmael. Grandmother of a grand nation.

But once I was nothing. A nobody. A throw-away.

Until God saw me, that is. Because that changed everything.

My jaw dropped.

I was used to odd requests from Sarai, my mistress. And I was usually happy to do them. Even though I had no choice—not really. My choice was always do my job or be sent off alone into the desert—something so terrifying I hated to even think of it.

But I always tried to keep a good attitude as I did even the worst jobs: as I scrubbed the pots that Sarai had gone to the bathroom in, as I beat her dirty clothes against rocks at the stream to clean them, and as I cooked and cleaned for her when she was healthy and when she was sick.

Age when she had Ishmael: Unknown. But she was probably between 20 and 30 years old.

Era: 2000 BCE

Even though she could be mean to me sometimes, I actually cared for Sarai. I even felt *bad* for her—truly— when I'd hold her as she cried (every month, for days on end) after discovering once again that she wasn't pregnant with the baby the Lord had promised her and her husband, Abram.

Sarai was a brokenhearted woman, and I understood that.

After all, I too wanted a child to hold in my arms, to sing to sleep at night, to laugh and play with in the cool desert evenings.

But that dream could never come true for me. I was a slave. I had no husband. And the Lord wasn't making *me* any promises.

But even though I understood my mistress's hurt and anger and desperation, never in my wildest dreams (or scariest nightmares!) did I think Sarai would concoct the plan she did.

Sarai wanted me, her servant, to give her a baby.

"You will have a child with my husband, Abram," she said, "and then you will give *me* your child. Your son will be the fulfillment of the Lord's promise."

I began to tremble. I didn't want to do this. I wanted my own husband someday, who would treasure me, love me. I didn't want to be with a man who would use me just to have a child.

"Please, ma'am," I said. "Please. No. You must wait and trust the Lord."

"No," Sarai said. "We must take matters into our own hands. And you must do as I say."

I ran back to my tent and collapsed on my bed. I cried and cried. I prayed the Lord would save me from this.

But the Lord didn't seem to hear or see me. Because not long after, Abram came to my tent and lay down next to me in my bed. And I became pregnant with his child.

And how I grew to love that child. Every day, as my body grew bigger and bigger, so did my love for the baby growing in me.

Something else grew inside me, though—something bad: I began to *hate* Sarai.

So I began to parade past her, reminding her what I had.

"Oh, ma'am," I would say, "my son is so strong. Too bad God doesn't give *you* a baby. Then you might know how wonderful it is to feel a baby kick inside you."

I said worse things too. Things I'm too ashamed to tell you. I was so mean. But for once in my life, I felt powerful. I'd never ever had anything that someone else wanted. Now I did.

But really, I was kidding myself, thinking I was powerful. Sarai still held the real power—and she showed it. Sarai wouldn't let me eat or sleep. She made me work harder than I ever had. When I didn't do something the way she liked, she'd whip me with a stick.

And then there was Abram. When Sarai told Abram that she could no longer stand the sight of me, he told her to do whatever she wanted to me. Beat me. Get rid of me. Whatever. It didn't matter to Abram: This man of God! Father of the child inside me!

So I ran away. I'd have rather faced life—and death—in the desert than live with Sarai's abuse.

I ran along the shores of the spring until my legs gave out from under me, until I collapsed in the hot sun.

That's where an angel of the Lord found me.

"Hagar, servant of Sarai," the angel said, crouching beside me, "why are you out here? Where are you going?"

"I'm running away from Sarai," I said. I couldn't contain my tears. They rolled down my face.

"I see," the angel said. "But you need to go back."

"I can't."

The angel wrapped her wings around me, lifted me up.

"Hagar," the angel said, "God has heard your misery. You will have a son and name him Ishmael. He will be a wild donkey of a man, a rabble-rouser, but God will give him many sons. His descendants will be a great nation. There will be too many to count."

I brought my hands to my stomach: *Ishmael.*

I said it again out loud. "Ishmael! That means 'God heard me.'"

The angel nodded.

God had given my son a name, so I gave God one.

"And the Lord is El Roi," I told the angel. "The God who sees."

Fast Facts

◇ Abram and Sarai both get a name change as the story goes on. You can read more about it in Genesis 17.

◇ A servant like Hagar was actually a slave. She was considered the property of her mistress.

◇ Hagar would've been one of many lower-class servants in Abram's household.

◇ In Hagar's time, families lived in large tents woven from goat hair or sheep's wool. Women wove the fabric, stitched the tents together, and repaired them. And the women set up and took down the tents when the community moved to find new places for their animals to graze.

God had heard and seen me! In my misery, God had been there. With me.

I ran back to Sarai.

My Ishmael was a wild donkey from the start. What a boy! What a delight! Nonstop energy and troublemaking. How I loved him. And so did Abram. He beamed with pride even as Ishmael played tricks on the other servants—or put snakes in Sarah's tent. (That's what God had changed her name to. And God had changed Abram's name to Abraham.)

In time, my mistress did have a boy of her own—Isaac. But I wondered if Abraham didn't favor Ishmael. At least for a while.

At least until that horrible day when our wild donkey took his teasing too far, as he made faces and did silly dances as little Isaac played.

Sarah flew into a rage.

"Enough!" Sarah turned to Abraham. "Get rid of that slave woman and her son! Ishmael doesn't deserve to be called your son or to share in Isaac's inheritance."

There was fire in her eyes.

Abraham approached Sarah, trying to calm her down.

"I'll talk to Ishmael," he said.

"No," said Sarah, "he must go."

Abraham lowered his head and walked to the tent.

Early the next morning, Abraham came to my tent. He carried a skin of water and a basket of fruit and bread and dried meat. How different it was that day than the first time he had visited me. And yet I shook with fear once again. What would become of me? Of us?

"I have prayed," Abraham said. "And Sarah is right. You must go."

I gasped. I thought the Lord would save me. I thought El Roi—the God who saw me!—would save me.

"Take Ishmael and go far away. There he will become a great nation because he is my son. And God promised me a son who would father a nation."

Abraham went over to Ishmael, placed a hand on his sleeping head, and wept. Then Abraham handed me the basket and the water and left without a word.

The food and water didn't last long. Wandering in the desert took every ounce of energy out of us.

After Ishmael sucked the last of the water from the skin, I told him to rest under a bush. I turned and walked away from him.

In reality, I couldn't bear to hear his cries or to watch him die.

Once God had heard me and my misery. Once God had seen me as I wept. I wondered if God could see and hear us now.

Get the Full Story
Genesis 16 and 21:8-21

I collapsed on the ground and sobbed. I had obeyed God. I had gone back to my mistress. God had promised me that my boy would lead a nation. And yet, here we were. About to die.

I heard a voice above me.

"Hagar, what's wrong?"

I gasped.

"Don't be afraid. God still sees you. God still hears. He heard your boy crying under the bush. Go to him! Take his hand! That wild donkey will one day be the head of a great nation!"

I rushed over to Ishmael and pulled him from the bushes. As I hugged him tight, Ishmael said, "Mama, look."

I opened my eyes. Before us stood a well, bubbling with fresh water. I ran to it and filled our skin and handed it to my boy.

We laughed as we drank and splashed the water all over ourselves.

God had seen us. God had heard us. *Ishmael. El Roi.*

And God continued to see us as my boy grew up, as he first picked up a bow and arrow and became a famous archer, as he married a woman from Egypt, as their children grew into a great nation.

Call me Hagar, the woman God saw and heard.

Think About It

Abram/Abraham and Sarai/Sarah are important people in the Jewish, Christian, and Muslim faiths. But they weren't always very nice to Hagar. What do you think about that?

God asked Hagar to do something scary—to go back to Sarai! Why do you think she did it?

Hagar learned that God saw and heard her. What are some ways you can tell that God sees and hears you?

Prayer Prompt

God sees and hears you too, no matter what. If you're not sure about that, ask God to help you feel God's presence and comfort more clearly.

Chapter 3

Leah

I have a complicated family.

First: even though some have said my eyes are "lovely" (whatever that means), I'm known as the ugly sister, as the girl no man wanted to marry. Ugh.

Then there's this: My sister, Rachel, and I share a husband, Jacob. Want to know why? Because my dad tricked Jacob into marrying me first.

Like I said, I have a complicated (and very embarrassing) family.

Well, my family would be much more embarrassing if it weren't for my amazing kids. And truly, they are *all*—all seven of them!—amazing. Believe me. I'm not just saying this because I'm their mother. They are amazing. And important. They are destined to do great things.

Like I said, *amazing*.

Sure, they'll make some mistakes in their lifetimes, but these kids are my everything. They gave me love. They gave me joy. And they gave me hope, when I had none of it.

My children are the reason I know that the God of Jacob loves me. They are the reason I know that God saw my humiliation. They are the reason I know God saw that Jacob would never, ever, ever love me.

But I'm getting ahead of myself. You should meet my kids—and hear what their names mean.

First, we've got Reuben, which means "God has seen my misery." (Because he did!) Then we have Simeon, which means "God hears me." Next is Levi, which means "attached." And then my boy Judah, whose name means "I will praise the Lord." That rounds out the first batch

Age: Probably 21. Many scholars think Rachel and Leah were twins and that Jacob met Rachel when she was the marriage-able age of 14.

Era: 1630–1500 BCE

Get the Full Story
Genesis 29:1-35

of kids.

Are you starting to see a theme to their names? My mother once joked that my kids' names sound like a prayer, a *lament,* actually, which is a sad or mad prayer that ends in praise. My mom may have been joking, but she was right! They are a prayer. And the prayers continue with the next three.

For years after Judah was born, I thought I was done having kids, but then God gave me three more children.

One right after the next, I had Issachar, Zebulun, and my beautiful Dinah. Their names mean "reward," "honor," and—how's this for my girl?—"avenged."

So maybe these last three were less about prayer and more about myself, but who can blame me?

Even with all the sons and the beautiful daughter I bore for Jacob, he loved Rachel the best. With each additional child, I thought maybe—just maybe—Jacob would learn to love me, feel attached to me, at least a little.

But Rachel had been the one he wanted long ago when he worked seven long years to win her hand from our father—only to be tricked into marrying me. Jacob went on to work *another* seven years to get Rachel as his bride. A man worked fourteen years—for free—to get to marry Rachel.

Imagine being that guy.

Now imagine being me. The ugly consolation prize.

But then imagine how I feel about God, who saw me, who heard me, who recognized that I was unloved. Imagine how it feels to know God cares about my tears, that God cares that I was so ashamed and embarrassed and unloved that God blessed me with what my sister most desired: children. God gave me so many children!

Of course, God is so good and generous that God heard Rachel's weeping too. God gave her two sons. And Jacob loved them more than he loved my sons.

Sigh.

Should I tell you the story of how Jacob hid Rachel

Fast Facts

◊ If Leah's story reminds you of Hagar, you're right! God sees, hears, and helps the lonely and unloved.

◊ Leah was the great-great-great-great-great-great-etc.-grandmother of Jesus. Jesus is sometimes referred to as the "Lion of Judah." That Judah is Leah's son!

◊ Some versions of the Bible refer to Leah's eyes as "weak" rather than "lovely." Kind of weird, isn't it? But people who study these things think the description is meant to convey a certain fragility, vulnerability, and tenderness about her.

◊ Not only did Leah share her husband with her sister; Jacob was also her first cousin!

◊ At the time, the custom was for the older sister to get married before the younger sisters. This is why Laban "tricked" Jacob. Some Jewish scholars think Leah was supposed to marry Esau, but she feared Esau, so her father was being kind by marrying her to Jacob.

and her sons when he thought his brother Esau was going to attack us? And how he put *me* and *my* children on the front lines to face the attack?

Perhaps another time. It's a crazy story. But let's just say Esau didn't attack us. God had worked peace and joy into Esau's life, and God had big plans for my kids—no matter where Jacob put them.

All this to say, God took me—an ugly, unloved woman—and made me mother of the nations: great-great-great-great-great-great-etc.-grandmother of a Savior, of Immanuel, which means "God with us."

And he is indeed.

Think About It

So much of this story seems strange to us now. A husband with two wives? Marrying your cousin? Because the customs of the ancient Hebrews aren't anything like ours (thank goodness!), it can seem like Leah's life is nothing like yours. But what about Leah and her life *do* you understand? Or what about her life sounds similar to your own?

What does it tell you about God that God pays attention to a woman like Leah who feels forgotten and unwanted?

What are some ways you might be part of what God is doing in the world?

Prayer Prompt

You probably know someone who feels like they're unloved or unlovable. Ask God to help you be someone who loves others well. What do you think that would look like for you?

Chapter 4

Miriam

Mother couldn't watch. I can't say I blamed her. Though we made the basket ship-shape, weaving the strands of papyrus as tightly as we could and spreading tar and pitch across the bottom and up the sides to keep it watertight, the Nile River was no place for a baby.

Which is exactly why
Pharaoh had ordered that
every newborn Hebrew
boy be thrown into the
Nile. Even *if* the baby
miraculously stayed afloat

Age when Moses was born: 11

Era: 1400–1300 BC

in the waters—with the crocodiles, hippos, and cobras always on the lookout for their next meal?—he wouldn't stand a chance.

Mother had tried to hide my brother, Moses, as long as she could, hoping that in the three months she kept him tucked tightly away in our hut, Pharaoh would change his mind.

But he didn't.

The order remained.

What could we do? We were Pharaoh's slaves. We had no power to fight him—even though that's what Pharaoh worried most about. His fear that our men would rise up and fight against him is the reason Pharaoh ordered the baby boys killed in the first place.

You'd think he would've wanted *all* the Hebrew boys and men killed, but of course, then he'd have no one to farm his lands, to build his buildings, to do his work. So he just went after the babies.

Which brings me back to my mother—who ran back to the hut in tears after placing her baby boy into the mighty Nile—and to my brother, whom I watched float away as I hid in the reeds.

I couldn't leave. I was prepared to run along the river

with his basket for as long as he floated. There was no way I could leave him. I wanted to give my mother good news, tell her he'd floated away safely. I decided not to tell her I could hear him crying.

As I crawled out from my hiding spot among the weeds ready to move downstream, I heard a rustling nearby. Worried it was a croc—already—I knelt back into the reeds and prayed.

"God, please," was all I could muster.

But when I opened my eyes, I realized it was no crocodile.

Get the Full Story
Exodus 2:1-10, Exodus 15 (Really, the entire book of Exodus.)

Pharaoh's daughter—the princess!—and her servants were wading in the river, not far from where I hid.

I panicked. What would they do if they saw the basket? Surely, the princess would command her servants to drown the boy.

I prayed again, "God, please!"

When I looked up, I saw the basket had floated into some reeds. I breathed a sigh of relief. If my brother stayed quiet, they might not notice.

But Moses squawked in the basket, and they all looked his way.

Pharaoh's daughter pointed to the basket and ordered her servant to bring it to her.

The princess opened the basket slowly, her face firm,

as though expecting a cobra to uncoil. But then she smiled.

"Oh, goodness," the princess said. "My sweet boy. What are you doing in a basket?"

Moses began to cry harder, and the princess reached for him, holding him tight against her body and rocking him.

"This is one of the Hebrew babies," the princess said. "He's afraid. And hungry."

I don't know what came over me. Looking back, it was a pretty dumb thing to do. After all, if the princess guessed why I was at the river and that it was my mother who had disobeyed Pharaoh by placing the baby in a basket instead of tossing him into the river, my mother might have been thrown into prison. Or worse—tossed into the river herself!

But I felt God nudge me into the open.

I had something important to do.

So I shot up out of the reeds.

"Ma'am," I said.

The princess jumped, and my brother jumped with her. He cried louder.

"Where did you come from, little fish?" she asked.

"I was just watching the river," I said. "But I can help."

"Help?"

"I can get one of the Hebrew women to nurse your baby for you. I know someone."

The princess looked down at the baby, smiled, and said, "Yes. I can't feed him. Go find someone who can."

I've never run faster in my life. The boys in town teased me as I passed.

"Mosquitoes under your tunic, Miriam?"

Normally, I'd have stopped to whack them, but I had no time. I had to get Mother.

"Mother! Mother!" I yelled as I rushed through the door. "Come quick. The princess found the baby! He's alive!"

Mother looked up from the bed. Her eyes were red, her cheeks splotchy.

"Don't tease me, Miriam," she said. "Let me be."

"I'm not teasing, Mother. I prayed to God and God heard me and the princess saw the baby in the basket and she heard him crying and cradled him and I said I could find her a Hebrew woman to feed him and she said to go and here I am and you have to come!"

At this point, I was pulling her arms so hard, I thought I'd tug them right off.

"We've got to go!" I said, finally hauling her to her feet.

And so Mother followed me. She kept up with me as we ran back to the river, where the princess still stood, rocking and cooing at my whimpering brother.

Mother paused and took a deep breath. I thought she'd collapse into tears again.

But instead Mother curtsied and said, "Your highness, this girl says you need someone to nurse a child. I can help you."

"Oh, thank you," the princess said. "I can tell already he is one special boy. One day he'll be a prince, a leader. But for now, he needs food. I will pay you for your service to me."

And the princess gave the baby a kiss on the head and handed him to my mother.

The boy stopped crying right away and began to settle into my mother's arms, rooting for milk.

The princess then put a hand on my head and thanked me.

She said, "I can tell that you are one special girl too. You are brave and helpful. Who knows? One day you may be a leader also."

She would turn out to be right about both of us! I grew to help my brother lead our people out of Egypt, across a parted sea,

Fast Facts

◊ **Miriam was a prophet, which was not considered unusual for women at that time. She was also musical! Prophets often used music to "induce trances," from which they'd hear prophecy.**

◊ **Miriam worked with Moses to free the Hebrew people from slavery under the Pharaoh.**

◊ **Miriam's mother was needed to nurse the baby not only because the princess couldn't do it—she hadn't given birth, so she wasn't producing milk—but because wealthy women often had servants nurse their babies for them.**

into a new land. The people would call me a prophet. But first, we had Moses to raise.

Moses stayed with us at our house for a few years. Then he returned to the princess and grew up in her home. He grew up a prince! Imagine that!—born a slave and he became a prince of Egypt!

But all along, he heard the stories of the Hebrew God, and one day, our God spoke to Moses from a burning bush, told him what he needed to do and who he was meant to be.

Moses was nervous—he didn't speak well and didn't think he could do it. But he did! My little brother, Moses, led our people out of Egypt.

And I ran alongside him the whole time.

Think About It

Why do you think Miriam stayed to watch her brother float away?

What was surprising about the way Pharaoh's daughter responded to the baby? Has there been a time when you jumped to a conclusion about how someone would react and they surprised you (in a good way)? What did you learn from that?

Miriam did lots of heroic things in this story—things that prepared her to lead the Israelites out of Egypt! How do you think the brave things you do in your everyday life might prepare you for your future?

Prayer Prompt

Ask God to help you be brave, quick-thinking, and willing to step up and act in the right moments.

Chapter 5

Rahab

My house was a good place to hide. It was built into Jericho's thick wall, with arched windows that made perfect "sneak-outs." More than one man had shimmied down the wall to make a fast exit into the dark desert night.

Plus, my neighbors were used to seeing men of all

ages, shapes, and sizes, from downtown Jericho or from out beyond the gates, walk through my doors at all hours.

Though it had caused quite the commotion when I opened up my home to entertain lonely men, my friends and family had grown used to the work I did. They mostly ignored me and the fact that I got paid to spend time with men and offer them companionship for an evening.

Age in story: Unknown. Probably late teens or early 20s, since her parents are still alive. Jewish tradition holds that she converted to Judaism at age 50.

Era. 1350 1250 BCE

Still, it wasn't the kind of work a respectable woman did. And I was embarrassed by it. I never wanted to be a "harlot," as many called me—either to my face or behind my back. But I was an unmarried woman from a poor family. How else could I expect to feed myself or my younger brothers and sisters back home? The money I sent them ensured that my little sisters would never end up like me.

I wasn't proud of the work I did. But I was proud I could help my family. I did what I had to do.

So the night the spies showed up at my door asking for help, I thought nothing of it. Little did I know that night would change the course of my life, my family's life—and all of history.

I rushed down the ladder and cracked open the door.

"Please," one of the men said, "may we come in?"

Normally the men who came to my door weren't so polite. They often shoved the door open, never asked. I wondered what was up.

I opened the door wider and waved them inside.

The men looked around quickly before ducking into my dark front room.

They weren't from Jericho. I could tell right away. They were travelers: their faces reddened from wind and sand, their voices cracking from thirst, their bodies worn and weary from what looked like years in the wilderness.

"Can you help us?" one of the men asked. "We can pay you."

I nodded.

"Of course," I said.

"This is going to sound crazy," one of them said. "But we need a place to hide."

"Your wives won't find you here," I assured them.

"No," one of the men laughed. "Not from our wives. From the king."

And then I realized who these men were. I had heard rumblings of Hebrew spies who had come to Jericho, scoping out our city ahead of their attack. And the Israelites weren't like our regular enemies, who fought with the same weapons we did.

We had heard the stories of what their God had done

for them—how their God had parted the sea and drowned the Egyptians in it. We could only imagine what their God would do to us.

And yet something in me wondered about the God they worshipped. I had prayed to our gods my whole life—for a husband, for food, for my family—and our gods never answered.

The Hebrew God parted seas and toppled Egyptian chariots for his people.

I wanted to be on their God's side.

"I can hide you," I said.

I rushed the men up the ladder to my room and used a broom to push up a ceiling tile that led to the roof. A rope fell through the open space as I pushed the tile aside.

"Follow me," I said as I pulled myself up the rope.

Once on the roof, I moved stalks of soggy flax I had set there to dry and tucked the men beneath them.

"Sorry for the smell," I said as they wriggled their noses along with their bodies, trying to get comfortable.

Fast Facts

◊ The Gospel of Matthew has a long list of names called a genealogy—like a family tree. Rahab is the mother of a man named Boaz. That makes her an ancestor of King David. Jesus was a descendant of David.

◊ Rahab would've dried flax under the hot sun to weave into ropes and cloth.

◊ Some scholars think Rahab married one of the spies. Others believe she married Joshua, though the Bible calls her husband "Salmon."

But then we all jumped when we heard pounding on the door two stories below.

I motioned the men to be silent and still. I shimmied back down the rope and pulled the tile closed behind me.

"One moment," I yelled from my room. "I'm not decent. I'll be down shortly."

Sweat poured down my face and back. I quickly toweled off before heading back down the ladder.

Once again, I cracked open the door.

Two of the king's soldiers pushed through (I recognized both of them) and asked to see the spies. The king knew they had come here.

If I turned the men in, I'd be rewarded beyond measure. I'd be able to leave this life once and for all.

But as I opened my mouth to answer, I thought of the Hebrew God who parted seas to save these people. I was on their side now. I had to trust that the God of the Hebrews was on mine. So I answered with a lie I have never once regretted.

"I'm so sorry, sirs," I said. "The king is right. Two travelers *were* here. But I had no idea they were spies! Goodness! To think I let them get away. They left just before dusk, before the gates closed. Perhaps you can still catch them if you go quickly! The king will reward you if you do! And so will I."

I smiled at the men. And they smiled back, before taking off running into the night, eager to catch up to the men I had hidden on the roof.

I closed the door and leaned against it, setting the bolt into place before climbing back up to the roof.

I moved the stalks out of the way and knelt before the men.

"I know who you are," I said. "And I know that if you are here, it's because your God has given you this city and this land. I've heard the stories of what your God has done. When news reached Jericho of how your God dried the Red Sea and how you destroyed your enemies, our hearts melted in fear. We're all terrified of you because your God is not only in heaven—God's here on earth with you.

"I will keep you safe and not say a word of what you are doing, but promise me that you and your God will keep me and my family safe when you come back. Do what your God says to do to Jericho, but promise me nothing will happen to my family."

The spies nodded and reached their hands forward.

"Our lives for your lives," they said.

And we made a deal. I would hang a red sash in my window when the Israelites returned. That would be the sign to the army that anyone in my home should be saved.

Later that night, the spies shimmied down the wall toward the hills, where the rest of the Israelites awaited their report.

Get the Full Story
Joshua 2

Not long after, I woke to the sounds of marching beyond the wall and of crying within.

The Israelite army was marching around our city. Everyone in Jericho knew what it meant. We all shook in fear.

Every day for six days, I ran to my father's house, begged him to bring my mother, my brothers, my sisters, our animals to my house. I promised him he would be safe. Not until the seventh day—not until the trumpets began to blast and the soldiers began to shout—did my father finally relent. We all ran through the streets, back to my house, where the red sash hung through the window.

As soon as we closed the door behind us, the walls began to crack and crumble around us.

"The roof!" I yelled and directed my family up the ladder, where we were met by an Israelite soldier.

My sister screamed. My father nearly fainted.

"I'm Rahab," I said to the soldier as he grabbed me.

"I know," he said. "We've been waiting for you. Tell your family to come this way. Quickly."

Each of us grabbed hold of a rope and scaled down what was left of the wall.

We'd not gone far when the solider yelled, "Run!"

And we did.

We didn't see the walls fall. But we felt the ground rumble and quake beneath us. We heard our former neighbors screaming and wailing as they got crushed by falling rock and as soldiers drew their swords and killed everyone.

Everyone.

Everyone but us.

The solider brought my family to Joshua, the leader of the Israelites. He took us into his home, made us—the poor refugees from Jericho—part of his family, part of his people.

And we made their God our God. The God who had parted the seas and toppled thick city walls, who had led the people out of slavery, had also saved me.

But the story didn't end there. The strangest part of my story happened centuries and centuries later.

God used me—a harlot, an embarrassment to her family, a nobody, a refugee—to be in the ancestral line of the great kings and the Savior of the world.

Imagine that.

Think About It

Rahab didn't have a good reputation in town. The type of work she did wasn't respectable. What does it tell you about God that God chose someone like Rahab do the important work of hiding the spies? Does it tell you anything about Jesus to know he is part of her family?

Rahab lied. Does it make a difference that she lied to protect others? What do you think about this situation?

Prayer Prompt

Who do you know who needs protection—from danger, from bullies, from gossip? How could you help that person or group of people feel safe? Ask God to help you to be willing to defend and protect others—even when it comes at a personal risk.

Chapter 6

Deborah

I am Deborah, mother of Israel,
 Prophet, judge, and poet.
 (If you've read my story,
You already know it.)
But I'll tell my story another way

So you can hear from my own mouth

Just what happened back in the day.

I rolled my eyes.

(Men! They can be so terrified!)

Poor Barak standing there shaking

In my court, a big man quaking.

Barak knew where he had to be—

If we wanted to set our people free.

But he wouldn't go alone, so "Please," he begged, "go with me."

"For sure, I'll go,"

I told him loud and clear.

"But if I go, you won't get the glory, my dear.

That'll go to a woman much braver than you.

But if you're cool with that, that's what we'll do."

Age when she became a leader: Probably 40 since the Jewish people lived in peace for 20 years under her rule.

Era: 1107–1067 BCE

So Barak and I gathered 10,000 men

We'd fight our captors, again and again

If we had to.

But I knew we wouldn't

Because the thing that
made Barak so scared

Was that he
thought God no longer
cared.

After all, we'd been
slaves for far too long.

It sure felt like God
had gone.

But no such thing.
God didn't go.

God was with us—
even in this show.

When I gave the
command for the
troops to fight,

I reminded them:
God goes ahead—
God'll show his might.

And show God did.

Though our enemies had iron chariots,

We won that battle, with just our lariats.

Before us and behind us, our enemies died.

Well, except for one who got away—or at least, tried.

Just as Barak got ready to sing his own praises

(Toot his own horn, for a war well won),

Fast Facts

◊ Deborah was a judge as well as a prophet. But she wasn't a judge in a courtroom. The judges we read about in the Bible were people who ruled over the tribes of Israel. Deborah is the only woman judge named. There weren't any kings or queens at the time, so the judges made the big decisions for the tribe.

◊ Though women in ancient Israel didn't have as many rights and opportunities as we do today, they seemed to have more opportunities than the women of the "heathen" nations around them.

◊ Deborah was married to Lappidoth, though we don't know anything else about her family.

I repeated what I'd told him—about whose glory would be sung.

Get the Full Story
Judges 4-5

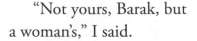

"Not yours, Barak, but a woman's," I said.

"Yours?" he guessed as he lowered his head.

"Not mine, Barak, but our story's not done.

One more needs to die and you'll see the glory won."

Because our enemy's leader had run off in the night

To the tent of Jael, where he thought he'd sleep without fright.

But Jael—his friend's wife—had another plan as she tucked him in tight.

"Sleep well," Jael said. "I'll keep watch by your bed!"

Then Jael drove a tent peg right into his head.

Long live Jael!

Brave sister of Israel!

Between her and me, the Lord set Israel free.

So never doubt what a woman can do.

With God on her side, nothing's impossible—it's true.

Jael and I, we rose above our station.

And know what? We saved a nation!

Think About It

What qualities do you see in Deborah's story that would have made her a good leader? What qualities do you have that would make you a good leader?

Deborah says God will deliver the Israel's victory into the "hands of a woman." What does that tell you about God's view of women?

Deborah was an honest-to-goodness warrior—with weapons and wars. But that's not the only kind of battles women of the Bible fought. Many were fighting for change. In what ways have you had to be a warrior? In what ways—or for what things—would you like to be a warrior?

Has anyone ever asked you to help them fight a "battle"? What was your response? "Certainly," like Deborah? Or something else? Why did you respond the way you did?

Prayer Prompt

Say a prayer about a "battle" you need to fight. Maybe you need to stand up for a friend. Maybe you need to stand up *to* a friend. Or maybe you need to fight for something in your school or your hometown. Ask God to help make you a warrior for the passions of your heart.

Chapter 7

Hannah

*D*ear God:

I'm not sure how much more of this I can take. Do you hear the way Peninnah makes fun of me for not having any children? She's so cruel.

My husband says she does it only because she knows he loves me the best, because I, not Peninnah, am his favorite

Age when she had Samuel: Unknown. Some believe she was unable to have children for 19 years after she reached puberty, so that would mean she was in her mid-30s when Samuel was born. Others believe she was much older.

Era: 1000 BCE

wife. He wonders why being his favorite isn't enough for me. He says his love is better than that of ten sons. But it's not true. Without a son, I am nothing.

God, you know that I would do anything for a child of my own. I'd give everything for a son to carry on our family name.

In fact, Lord most high, if you give me a son, a boy, I will dedicate him to you. He will never drink or smoke or cut his hair but will be your servant always.

Praise to you,

Hannah

Dear God:

I was mad when Eli the priest accused me of being drunk. Drunk! In the temple! How dare he accuse me of that when I was pouring out my soul to you. I can't help that my words slurred as I cried.

Of course, I told him as much, and Eli apologized. As he should! And I wonder if his words didn't stir something in you, God. I've prayed for a son for so long. But only now that Eli blessed me, asking that you, God, might grant my *petition, do I dare hope that this stirring I feel in my womb, that the sickness I feel every morning, is actually a child.*

May it be, Lord; may it be.

Praise to you,

Hannah

Dear God:

Hallelujah! Hallelujah! Hallelujah!

I'm pregnant! You heard my cries. Thanks to be to God!

Praise to you,

Hannah

Dear God:

A boy! My son! My beautiful Samuel. We named my boy this because "I have asked him of the Lord."

He is yours, God, more than he is mine. May he live a life worthy of you, God. May my Samuel rise to do mighty things.

Thank you! Thank you! Thank you!

Praise to you,

Hannah

Fast Facts

◊ *Hannah* means "favor" or "grace."

◊ *Samuel* means "God has heard."

◊ Hannah wasn't part of Jesus' family tree, but her son Samuel would appoint the first two kings of Israel: Saul and then David, who was an ancestor of Jesus.

◊ The Bible says Hannah brought Samuel to the temple when he was weaned. Scholars aren't sure if this means when he was technically weaned from nursing, around age three, or when he was weaned from needing his mother—maybe when he was somewhere between six and twelve. Either way, he was young.

Dear God:

Samuel is getting so big—but thankfully, not too big to still need his mother when he cries out in the night or when he scrapes his knees. And I confess I'm so glad. I promised his life would be dedicated to you, and I will bring him to the temple when he's old enough to be away from me. But when on earth is that? How will I know? Lord, help me.

Some days I regret the promise I made. Every day I wish you'd release me from it. But never—not for one day—do I regret my boy, Samuel. And never—not for one day—will I stop praying for him.

God, help me.

Praise to you,

Hannah

Dear God:

Today is the day I have both dreaded and prayed for.

Today we bring a three-year-old bull and our boy to the temple to offer to you. The bull will be a sacrifice. Our boy will be your servant.

I worry so much about leaving Samuel at the temple with Eli that sometimes I've wondered if the bull isn't the lucky one here. Certainly, leaving Samuel behind will feel like death to me.

God, you lent me Samuel for these years. You've made me happier than I ever imagined being. And now, God, I give him back to you. Be with my boy. Be near him. Don't let him feel afraid. Don't let him forget me. Don't let him ever think for one moment that I gave him up. Let him understand that you are the one who gave him up for me these years and now I'm just giving him back.

Let Eli and Eli's sons be good to Samuel. Let them take care of him.

Make him a good boy. Make him a good man. God, let him grow up in your presence.

Praise to you,

Hannah

Dear God:

I left Samuel with you. My heart broke. It was harder than I thought.

But you gave me courage. You gave me strength.

It's true what they say: There is no other god like you. You

∞∞∞∞∞∞∞∞∞∞

Get the Full Story
1 Samuel 1 and 2:1-11

∞∞∞∞∞∞∞∞∞∞

are my Rock.

You make the weak strong. You make the poor rich. You may let us struggle, but you raise us up. You lift us from the dust, from the dry ground we cry on.

You guard us. You protect us from our enemies.

Be with my boy. Be with me.

May the words of Eli once again come true: May you repay me with children for the gift of my son.

Praise to you,

Hannah

Dear God:

You were with me once again as I brought Samuel his robe. Every year as I approach the temple, my heart leaps and breaks all at once. I am so proud of my son, of the young man of God he is becoming, of the way he hears you calling him in the night, of the way he listens to you.

Thank you for not letting him forget me. Thank you that he still loves me. And thank you for hearing Eli's prayer all those years ago and for giving me more children. Thank you for my four sons and my two daughters.

And thank you, thank you, thank you for allowing my Samuel to grow up in your presence even though he cannot

grow up in mine.
    Praise to you,
    Hannah.

Think About It

There are lots of stories about women in the Bible who pray to have a baby. Why do you think these stories are important?

Hannah made a "deal" with God. Normally, we don't think doing this is a good way of praying. After all, God doesn't "need" anything from us. But God gave Hannah what she asked for. What might have been special or different about Hannah's prayer?

What do you think it was like for Hannah to leave her son at the temple? What do you think it was like for Samuel?

How do you feel about Hannah in this story? What about Eli?

Prayer Prompt

Hannah kept a promise that required her to make a huge sacrifice. Ask God to help you be a person who keeps promises and lives up to what God asks of you, even when it's hard.

Chapter 8

Naomi and Ruth

R uth steps through the front door, wipes her bare feet
on the mat, and sets down her wheat-filled pack.

Naomi: Shhhhhh, Obed's asleep.

Ruth's age when she married Boaz: Probably 40. Boaz was probably 80!

Naomi's age when Ruth married Boaz: Probably 60.

Era: 1300 BCE

Ruth: [*Whispers*] Sorry! Thanks for watching him for me. Harvest time makes things crazier than normal.

Naomi: You know I love to be with Obed. It's like I have my sons back. Feels like a million years ago that I was cradling them . . .

Ruth: Some days it does feel like we've lived two lives, doesn't it? One filled with such despair, and this one, with such hope, such promise.

Naomi: Well, those days back when I was raising my boys, when I watched them grow—and watched you and Orpah marry them!—weren't all bad. We had good times too.

Ruth: Of course. We had great times. But it's hard to forget the sadness. And the fear! We had no idea how we would survive when they died! I understood why you wanted me to call you "Bitter."

Naomi: [*Laughs*] Oh, you understood, did you? Then why did you never call me that?

Ruth: How could I? It's a terrible name!

Naomi: [*Laughs again*] Don't make fun of me, Ruth.

Ruth: I'd never do that, Old Bitter.

Naomi: Well, I'm certainly not bitter now. But back

then, I was so angry at God for allowing my husband and sons to die. How could he have done that to me? How could he have done that to you and Orpah?

But you know what? Even in the middle of being so mad at God, I could tell the Lord was with me. He never let me forget he was there. And God did that through you.

Ruth: Through *me*?

Naomi: Of course! It was your words—about my people being your people, my God being your God—that reminded me just who my God was.

I may have been mad at God for taking my boys and my husband, but my God *was* a rescuer. My God was a redeemer, one who could make old things new and wrong things right. My God led our people out of slavery in Egypt and into the Promised Land.

And once again, God rescued and redeemed us. He led us out of desperation and into hope.

Did I ever thank you?

Ruth: You thanked me for coming with you.

Naomi: But for those words? Did I thank you for reminding me who my God—who *our* God—was?

Ruth: [*Smiles*] I think you just did. But you have it in reverse. *I* need to thank *you*. After all, you were the one to show me who your God was. Had

Get the Full Story

The Book of Ruth

Fast Facts

◊ **Ruth was Moabite. Naomi was her mother-in-law. Naomi and her husband and sons had moved to Moab during a famine in Bethlehem.**

◊ **Some scholars believe what Ruth learned about God would've been passed down to her son (Obed) and to his son (Jesse) and to his son (King David). David's psalms echo what Ruth learned.**

◊ **Even though Naomi's own children had died, when Ruth had Obed, according to custom, Naomi's family line was restored.**

◊ **Ruth and Naomi lived in a time when a woman with no husband or sons to take care of her had very few options for survival. She could be a slave, marry herself off to someone new, or struggle to survive on her own.**

◊ **Ruth would have been considered an outsider. She was part of a different ethnic group than Naomi and had every reason to go back to her family when her husband died. Instead, she stayed with Naomi, and together, they found a way to survive.**

you not told me the stories of God and his people, I might not have followed you. I may have returned to my parents and to my old gods.

But I could see your trust—even when you were Old Bitter Boots.

Naomi: Well, I'm not bitter anymore. What a life God has restored to us! God has restored my family through you, through Boaz, through dear little Obed. [*Rocks Obed*] Shhh, shhh, shhh, back to sleep, sweetheart. And I know God will do great things through this child.

Ruth: I'm sure he will. Obed's got you as a nanny, teaching him all your crafty ways.

Naomi: Crafty! What do you mean?

Ruth: Bitter Mama, you know *exactly* what I

mean. When you sent me out to collect wheat in Boaz's field, you knew what you were doing.

Naomi: We were hungry! What else were we to do? How was I to know Boaz would like you? Just because I knew the way my son adored you, it didn't mean all the men in my family would think that way.

I did, however, expect Boaz to take care of you—of us—and he did, by offering you not just the scraps, but full bushels of wheat.

Ruth: And what did you expect him to do when I went to the threshing room floor that night, when you told me to uncover his feet and then lie next to them?

Naomi: [*Laughing*] Okay. I *did* think that would get his attention. And it did!

But the important part is God. Maybe I was crafty, but God was the grand-crafter of all of this. God saw us in our misery and saved us.

And now, dear Obed, may our people always be your people, and our God always be your God.

Ruth: [*Leans in to kiss Obed*] Amen.

Think About It

What do you think Ruth risked by following Naomi and not returning to her parents?

After her husband and sons died, Naomi wanted to be called Mara—or "Bitter." How does your name define who you are?

Prayer Prompt

Families can be pretty messy, but sometimes we have to stick up for or stick with our families even when they bug us. Ask God to help you have the courage to stand up for the people in your family, even when they embarrass or disappoint you.

Chapter 9

Queen Esther

King Xerxes ruled the world—or nearly so. His kingdom stretched far across the globe, from India to Persia, from ocean to ocean, across rivers and seas and deserts and mountains.

Age when taken to the
palace: 14

Age when made queen: 15

Era: 492–460 BCE

King Xerxes commanded his people—of all shapes and sizes, of all religions and cultures—from a golden throne that sparkled with rubies and emeralds and sapphires.

When the king gave orders, people jumped to obey. Because if they didn't, if they ignored even the tiniest or most terrible command, Xerxes came up with terrifying punishments.

People knew better than to disobey King Xerxes.

Or at least, I did.

But one day, smack-dab in the middle of a wild, wild party that lasted seven days, King Xerxes asked his wife, Queen Vashti, to wear her finest crown and her newest gown and dance for his friends. The king wanted to show off his beautiful queen.

Vashti didn't like this order. It made her feel used. She wasn't like the king's golden throne—an object to be admired. She was the queen! So Vashti said no. To the king. (Can you imagine?) Queen Vashti disobeyed a terrible command.

When King Xerxes heard this, his face reddened. His ears burned. He was furious. And embarrassed! He roared a command that would show everyone he was still boss: "Vashti is no longer queen. Bring me her crown."

The party guests gasped. The king smiled. Until he realized he had a problem. The king had to find another queen.

So King Xerxes sent his servants across his kingdom. They searched from India to Persia, from ocean to ocean. They crossed rivers and seas and deserts and mountains, looking for the most beautiful women.

And (I'm a little embarrassed to admit this—I hate to brag), one of the women they found was me.

I'd heard stories of the king's servants rumbling across the land, breaking down doors, and taking women—girls, really—from their homes to meet the king.

And every day my cousin Mordecai and I would pray that I wouldn't be taken.

Still, he told me, "If you must go, just remember: God goes with you."

Then one day, we heard a *thump, thump, thump* on our door. We both froze.

When the messengers burst through the door and saw me, *they* froze. I didn't know why, but I didn't like it. I'd never felt so afraid.

"We're here on orders of His Majesty, King Xerxes," a servant said. "You must come with us."

Mordecai took a step forward, his fists raised. Ever since my parents died, he'd loved and protected and raised me as his own. He wasn't going to stop now. I loved him for that. But I reached forward and grabbed Mordecai, terrified of what would happen if we disobeyed the king. So, even though I shook and shivered with fear, I obeyed a terrible command.

"Okay," I told the servant. "I will go."

As I hugged a sobbing Mordecai goodbye, I whispered, "And God goes with me."

The servants lifted me onto the back of a wagon. Mordecai, bless him, ran after us all the way to the palace, where they locked all the girls they'd gathered in rooms filled with perfumes and lotions, shampoos and brushes, fancy robes and shimmery jewelry.

They took us because we were beautiful, but the king wanted us made even *more* beautiful. So every day, for six months, servants unclicked the lock on my door to yank through my hair, scrub rough skin off my hands and feet and elbows, and rub oil on my skin.

Then, every day, for *another* six months, the servants unbolted the door and covered me with perfume, rubbed my cheeks with red clay, and darkened my eyes with black kohl.

I hated this. It made me feel used. I missed Mordecai. I missed home.

But every day, as the servants tugged and yanked and rubbed, I closed my eyes and remembered what Mordecai had told me: God was with me.

So I asked God to help. To make me brave even though I was scared. To help me use my brain even though I was confused. And I asked God to stay close beside me.

Finally, the day came for me to find out if the king found me beautiful enough to be his queen or if I would be cast out of the palace or, worse, kept as a servant.

As I walked down the long, dark hallway toward the king's chamber once again, I shook and shivered with fear. With each step, I prayed: *God, go with me.*

When the servants threw open the heavy wooden doors to the King's chamber and announced me, everyone in the room froze. Including the king.

Get the Full Story
The Book of Esther

I wasn't sure what this meant.

But King Xerxes smiled and snapped for his servant.

"The crown," he ordered. A servant rushed away and returned with a shimmering golden crown, dotted with rubies and diamonds and sapphires. The king brought it to me. I knelt, and the king set the crown on my head.

The king declared that day a holiday and threw a huge party to celebrate me, his new queen. I wasn't so sure it was something worth celebrating.

But God had gone with me. Just as Mordecai had. When he heard from his spot at the palace gate that I'd been made queen, he cheered. But his cheering didn't last long. Because just after I was made queen, Mordecai overheard two men planning to *kill* King Xerxes.

Mordecai sent me a letter. I quickly warned the king. The men were arrested and the king was saved. Mordecai was a hero!

But that didn't mean everyone liked Mordecai.

One of the king's best friends, Haman, hated Mordecai. Haman had gotten the king to decree that everyone in the kingdom should bow down to *Haman*. Mordecai refused. He bowed only before the God of the Hebrew people. And neither Haman nor the king bowed to our God.

So Haman made a terrible plan. To punish Mordecai, Haman asked the king to kill all the Jewish people in the kingdom—starting with Mordecai.

The king—who was busy celebrating me—agreed. But he didn't know I was Jewish. So King Xerxes gave the terrible command to kill all the Jewish people in his kingdom.

But Mordecai had a plan. Not long after the king's command, I received another letter from my cousin. The letter said:

Dearest Esther:

You must go to the king and ask him for mercy.

God made you for this moment. He made you beautiful and brave so you could save your people.

Mordecai

I knew he was right. But I was more afraid than ever. The king had another terrible rule: Anyone who visited him without permission would die. Including the queen. And I didn't have permission.

But I remembered: God was with me! So I wrote back to Mordecai:

My dear Mordecai:

Yes, I will go to the king.

Ask our people to fast and pray for me.

If I die, I die. But I will try.

Queen Esther

I tried not to imagine the terrifying punishment I might face as I put on my best robe and my finest crown, as I perfumed my neck and dusted red clay on my cheeks,

Fast Facts

◇ Some ancient beauty treatments involved burning spices near the body so they'd be absorbed into the person's skin and clothes.

◇ God is never actually mentioned by name in the book of Esther.

◇ Esther's birth name was Hadassah, which means "myrtle tree."

◇ Purim is a Jewish holiday, celebrated still today, based on the story of Queen Esther. Jewish people read the story of Esther, cheering for Mordecai and Esther and booing whenever Haman's name is mentioned.

and as I made the long walk to the king's chamber.

But this time, when the doors to his chamber opened, I did not freeze. Nor did I shake or shiver with fear.

"My king," I said, "may I have a word?"

The room stilled as the king looked up from his game.

I knew one of two things would happen: Either he would reach his golden scepter toward me and grant permission. Or he would order my death.

I took a deep breath.

The king looked me up and down. His lips pulled up into a smile.

The king reached for his scepter—and held it to me!

Xerxes smiled as he said, "My dear, what do you need? Ask for half the kingdom and I'll give it to you!"

But I didn't want his kingdom. I wanted the king to change his terrible order. He wasn't going to like this.

I began to cry and fell at his feet.

"My king," I said, "you ordered that all Jews be killed. This means that the man, Mordecai, who saved your life will be killed, as he is a Jew. And it means *I* will be killed as well, as I am a Jew."

Once again, the king's face reddened. His ears burned. He was furious. And embarrassed!

But this time, he didn't ask for my crown. He asked for his old friend Haman's head.

Then the king issued a new order that said the Jews would live.

I stood up and smiled. God was with me. And God had saved my people.

Afterward, the whole kingdom threw a party to celebrate what I had done. But really, whether the people knew it or not, they were celebrating what *God* had done.

Think About It

The story of Queen Esther is really a story of two brave queens. What did Queen Vashti do that was brave? Why do you think she refused the king? Was it worth it?

Sometimes people have turned the story of Queen Esther into a "fun" story about beauty pageants and becoming a princess. What do you think about that?

Esther went from being relatively poor to living in a palace. Why does she seem unhappy about this change?

Prayer Prompt

Each of us is called to step up and speak out against things we know are bad or wrong. Ask God to help you recognize opportunities in your life to step up. Pray that God helps you act in your time.

Chapter 10

Mary

My story is one of the most famous ever told. Surely you've heard it. Surely you know the part about me, Mary, the young girl, the maiden, the *virgin,* from Nazareth. You know—the one who was visited by an angel and was told she would bear God's Son?

Age when Mary had Jesus:
13 or 14

Era: 14 BCE–40 CE

That's me. That's my crazy story.

And whenever I tell it—or refer to it—people ask, "What was that like?"

"What do you mean, *What was that like?*" I always want to say. "What do you think? It was terrifying! In every way!"

The angel was terrifying. The very idea that I could be pregnant without even being married was terrifying. The thought of telling my fiancé, Joseph—and oh, the thought of telling my *father*—was terrifying.

And yet? To be asked to carry the Son of God, to take on this miraculous task? *That* was magnificent.

And surely you all know what happened after that: the story of Jesus' birth.

At Christmas, people tell the story of Joseph and me traveling to Bethlehem to register our family. Everyone talks about me giving birth to my son, Jesus, in a stable, surrounded by noisy, stomping donkeys and sheep covered in hay and stable-gook. Children sing of us being visited by shepherds (who were also noisy, stomping, and covered in hay and stable-gook, now that I think of it) and kings.

But even still—even when all people think they know, still they ask me: "What was *that* like?"

What can I say? It was scary, yes (any new mom can

tell you having a baby is scary). But it was also glorious. Amazing. A baby—no matter how he or she comes—is a gift. Always. And Jesus was the very best gift.

Fewer people ask about our years as refugees in Egypt, run off by a king who wanted our boy dead. Or about when we came back home to Nazareth. But I wish they would ask, because it was hard. Really hard. Nobody in my hometown believed my story of the angel's visit or my miraculous pregnancy. Everyone assumed I'd made the whole thing up.

So I'd hear neighbors and former friends whisper behind my back. Everywhere I went, people would snicker and roll their eyes at me. I'd always shuffle away, little Jesus toddling along at my side, tilting his head at people's cruelty, squeezing my hand a little tighter.

How I loved that boy.

But as I raised Jesus—and his brothers and sisters—the whispers died away. After all, Jesus was such a wonderful boy. Different, for sure, but great. Everybody said so. After all, it was hard to miss his kind way with animals, the way he'd stop to pet the lambs and speak so sweetly over them, and the way he tended to injured birds. It was hard not to appreciate the way he included all the neighborhood kids—especially the shy ones or those who had trouble keeping up—in the games. And it was hard not to be dazzled by how quickly he learned the Scriptures and understood their ancient words well enough to talk with the rabbis—Jesus was at once challenging and respectful, in the way only a great student and scholar can be.

People do ask me about these years. Who doesn't want to know what it was like to raise the Son of God?

I suppose my answer is the same as any mother trying to do the best she can. It was hard. It was good. It was a challenge. It was a thrill. Raising Jesus was a joy I'd never known.

But there was something else, something that's harder to talk about. Something certainly no one asks about.

Because even on our best, happiest days, I'd worry. I'd worry about loving him as much as I did. I'd worry because I knew that whatever it was God had sent him to do would be dangerous. It would "pierce my soul," as the prophet Simeon told me back in the temple when Jesus was only eight days old.

How could sweet little Jesus break my heart? How could he pierce my soul? I couldn't imagine when he was a child, but as he grew and started traveling and teaching, I began to fear the worst.

As soon as Jesus began gathering disciples and preaching a message of love, I realized not everyone liked what he had to say. Not everyone approved of who he healed and when. Not everyone liked the different kind of peace Jesus offered. Not everyone wanted to be told to love our enemies (the Romans?!?) as well as our neighbors. Not everyone wanted to hear that the poor and the meek among us were the blessed ones. Nobody wanted to hear that we should give more to the poor and worry less about ourselves.

But most of all, not everybody wanted to hear Jesus claiming to be the Son of God, the Messiah. Certainly not the religious leaders of our day.

Of course, plenty of people did clamor to hear and believe what Jesus said. They were the ones who saw the miracles he performed, who experienced the great welcome he offered everyone in his presence, who felt the acceptance and mercy in his very glance. Others thought he would lead a revolution against the Roman government and that the Jewish people would finally be in charge, the way God had promised we would.

Jesus gained a following, and that only bothered the leaders more and more.

And one day, a sword did "pierce my soul," just as the prophet had said.

Fast Facts

◊ Mary is in the line of Christ—obviously. Some scholars believe she was also in the line of David—though there is some debate, as her cousin Elizabeth was in the priestly line of Levi.

◊ Mary is known by many names: the Blessed Mother, the Virgin Mary, Our Lady, the Madonna (which is from the Italian for "my lady").

◊ Mary is the subject of countless paintings, many of them considered masterpieces.

◊ Jewish girls were considered women when they were 12 years old plus one day.

◊ Jewish boys became men at 13.

◊ Men were expected to marry between 18 and 20 years old. But women typically married much younger. Mary was probably not much older than you!

That was the day I heard "Crucify him!" shouted from the streets. The day I saw Jesus dragged and whipped and beaten. The day I saw my son's broken and bleeding body dragging that cross toward Golgatha.

"What was that like?" some ask me.

The very worst. The worst thing you can imagine. I'm not sure there's an emotion for me screaming, crawling after Jesus in the street, begging for them to take me instead.

Get the Full Story

Matthew, Mark, Luke, and John

(See especially: Matthew 1-2 and Luke 1-2.)

I'm not sure there are words for the scene of me collapsing with the other Marys at the foot of the cross, of us weeping and moaning below his precious feet, the ones I'd kissed and cradled that night he was born.

What I wouldn't have given to go back . . . to be holding him again . . . to be visited by the shepherds. What I wouldn't have given to go back to those nights I snuggled him to sleep and prayed over him. What I wouldn't have given to giggle again together when we started our prayers with "Father, into your hands I commit my spirit." (All good Hebrew children prayed those prayers. Not all good Hebrew children were literally praying to their *father*.)

And in the moment Jesus whispered his final words on the cross, he *did* bring me back: "Father," Jesus said on that cross, "into your hands I commit my spirit."

When Jesus died, part of me did too.

My son—Immanuel, God with us—was no longer with me.

But you probably also know that my story doesn't end there. Even though during that Sabbath, from that Friday sundown to Saturday sundown, I thought it had.

As he was dying, Jesus had asked if God had forsaken him. That was how I felt: forsaken. By God. By the God who had asked me to carry this child. By the God to whom I'd said yes all those years ago. By the God I loved.

But then I remembered: those words—"My God, my God, why have you forsaken me?"—were so familiar. The beginning of a psalm—a lament—that ended with a great promise, with the words "He has done it." And I wondered . . . just what would God do?

And then Mary Magdalene showed up, screaming with joy.

"I've seen Jesus!" she said. "He's alive!"

God had done it.

When Jesus rose from the dead, I did too.

God wasn't done with my Jesus, and God wasn't done with me either.

So what's it like to be me? The mother of Jesus, the Son of God?

It's a *blessing.*

I am blessed.

That's the only word I know that captures a life with

Jesus. Because it's the only word that somehow takes the wonderful and the terrifying, the joyous and the hard, the heartbreaking and the hope-filled, and turns it into the so, so good, into something—everything—worth living for.

Think About It

Mary was just a young girl from a small town, but she is a central part of the story of our faith. What do you think about that?

Mary calls herself "blessed"—and yet her life was not easy. She was not rich. She was not powerful. How does Mary's use of that word help you understand what a blessing is?

Why do you think Mary said yes to the angel's message that she would have this baby?

Prayer Prompt

Ask that God bless your life—and make you a blessing to others.

Chapter 11

Mary and Martha

Mary's Journal Entry # 476

Ugh. My sister is driving me nuts! Again.

"Pick up your sandals, Mary." "We need more

eggs, Mary." "Sweep off the porch, Mary."

All day long, that's all I hear.

You'd *think* after Jesus himself told her to *stop* nagging me because I was doing the "better thing" (by listening to him teach) and she was doing the *worse* thing (by serving the food) that she'd stop. But does she? Um, no.

Martha just keeps going. And gets worse! Now, not only does she freak out about our house being "company ready" all the time, but she's obsessed with making sure we always have fresh bread and dried fish and jugs of water and wine on hand—in case friends stop by unannounced.

Which they do. I can't tell you how many mornings I've gotten up early to read and write, only to find another of Jesus' friends fast asleep on a mat on our floor.

So, I guess it is good that I got my sandals off of the sofa then. I suppose it's nice that they have a clean place to rest and something to eat when they wake up. Jesus keeps them moving pretty quickly when they're on the road.

And I'll admit: I'm pretty proud when I hear people talking around Bethany about how Martha is always ready to offer a meal to those who need one. People show up looking worn and skinny at our house at all hours. And Martha is always ready. She's quick to find them a spot at our table and to whip up food that brings the color back to their cheeks and the life back to their eyes.

Her acts remind me of Jesus, actually. The way he brought our brother back from the dead.

I don't know. Jesus did say that listening to him was better than cleaning. But now that I think about it? Martha *has* been listening to Jesus. And she's been living like him too.

Ugh. My sister is the best.

Martha's Day Calendar Entry #37.6

To Do:

√ Wash chamber pot

√ Sweep living room

√ Sweep loft

√ Make up spare bed

√ Start soup stock

√ Bake bread

√ Mend rug

√ Pay taxes

Feels good to get that done! I can finally stop for breakfast. Of course, Mary has been up for hours with me. But has she been helping? Of course not. She's sitting there, sprawled on the sofa reading one of Daddy's

Get the Full Story

Luke 10:38-42

old scrolls. She's lucky he's not alive to see her. Daddy used to get so mad at her, trying to sit and listen to him as he taught his students. And the questions she'd ask at dinner! She never stopped asking, even though his answers were always the same: "Mary, go help your mother and sister in the kitchen."

And then he'd reference that old prayer where he thanked God for not making him a woman. He'd laugh, but Mary never would. She didn't think it was funny. Looking back, I guess it wasn't.

But Mary never knew her place. Daddy was just trying to help her, really. What good does it do a girl like Mary to ask such questions, to sneak off to read and try to learn? What man would want to marry a girl like that? Certainly not any of Lazarus's friends or any of the fine Jewish men here in Bethany.

She never learned. Well, about that: Mary kept trying to learn, kept trying to sneak into the synagogue, trying to sneak off with Daddy's scrolls. She'd spend hours reciting Scripture, perfecting her memory work, whatever she could. Mary never gave up. She never let go of the

Fast Facts

◊ **Mary sitting at Jesus' feet would've been shocking to the disciples! It wasn't something respectable women did.**

◊ **Martha's name means "lady" or "mistress," which suits well her role as lady of the house.**

◊ **Mary was praised twice in the gospels for her devotion to Jesus.**

◊ **Mary and Martha were the only two women the Bible says Jesus loved— they were his dear friends.**

idea that God wanted her to learn about our sacred texts, to study as a way of becoming a better person.

I guess it paid off.

After all, Jesus *did* tell Mary she was doing the better thing. Better than I, he meant. I'm not going to lie—it stung when Jesus said that. In front of everyone. I was half-tempted to run back into the kitchen and cry, maybe "accidentally" drop a dish or two.

But then I caught Jesus' eye and I realized something. Jesus wasn't telling me that I did was wrong or bad. Goodness. No one looked forward to one of my meals more than Jesus. No one was more grateful or appreciative of the warm loaves and grilled fish after a long day than he was.

But not many appreciate Mary. She is a terrible cook, a terrible housekeeper. She couldn't mend a torn robe to save her life. Mary never knows where we keep the extra loaves when hungry people come looking.

But Mary is a good learner. She has the sharpest mind around. Mary could read the Torah and listen to Jesus—pondering, analyzing, questioning—all day long. That's her great gift to the world. And Jesus told her it was better that she use her gift than help me with mine.

No man had ever once let Mary sit at his feet and learn—not our father, not the other rabbis—but Jesus did. He welcomed her. He taught her. He didn't make jokes about her questions.

Probably that's why she poured all that perfume at his feet (without regard for what a mess it made!!!!). Mary wanted to honor Jesus as he had once honored her. Jesus had made her feel special for the first time in her life. Like she was made right.

And she was. She is.

My sister is the best.

Think About It

Why do you think Jesus thought what Mary did was better?

What do you think about the roles each of these sisters played in their household? What was important about what each woman did?

Who are you more like: Mary or Martha? What could you learn about yourself from each of these women?

Why do you think Jesus treated women differently (better!) than other men did in those days? What does that tell you about what God thinks about women and girls?

Prayer Prompt

Sometimes it's tempting to act like someone you're not. Ask God to help you use your gifts and to live as the person you were made to be.

Chapter 12

Mary Magdalene

Mary.

In my lifetime, I've heard my name said lots of different ways.

Age at Jesus' resurrection:
Unknown

Era: 30-35 CE

When I was little, my mother used to say it nicely. She'd stretch it out, sing-song it a bit, especially when she rocked me to sleep.

My father said it more sharply. Two quick syllables pierced the air and scared me—especially after he came home late at night, after drinking too much.

By the time I was a teenager, most people would raise it at the end. Like my name was a question. "Mary? What are you doing?" "Mary? Why are you doing that?" "Mary? Stop it."

I had a few troubles. I was weird. I was different. I was difficult.

But there was something worse than the way other people began calling my name in public.

I had other people—things really—calling my name from *inside* my mind. The way these voices in my head said my name made me feel worthless. Helpless. Hopeless.

Those were fitting words, really, because even though my name doesn't have an "s" anywhere in it, my name would slither and linger as the voices whispered it again and again. They told me I wasn't lovable. That I was no good. That I would never, ever be anything other than helpless. Hopeless.

I'd try to resist the voices. I'd hold my knees tight up to my chest, rock back and forth, and hum to myself. I was desperate to drown the whispers. When the humming and rocking failed, I'd try screaming.

Then I'd hear my name in a whole new way.

"Mary," people would say, shaking their heads and tsk-tsking my very presence. I heard them talk about the shame I brought my family—my good, upstanding family from Magdala. I'd hear them wonder what would become of me. I'd hear them bet my parents hoped I would just die.

I hoped that too.

But then one day, I met a man. His name was Jesus. And when he said my name, when he said, "Mary," he said it with a smile. Jesus smiled at me, at my name. And as he did, the voices in my head shrilled one last time and then grew silent. Dead silent.

Jesus said my name, and suddenly, my thoughts were my own again. No one in my head told me I was terrible. No one told me to lash out or scream. No one told me how dumb I was, how ugly I was, how bad I was.

Jesus called my name and told me I was beloved—by God. Jesus called my name and told me I was healed and I was worthy of love. I was good.

I followed him everywhere. If he could quiet the voices in my head, imagine what he could do for the whole world!

As Jesus healed the sick, raised the dead, gave dignity to the worthless and hope to the oppressed, I marveled at what this man could do. His love. His grace. His mercy.

They knew no boundaries.

Well, up until the day he died. Then it seemed all was lost. Forever.

But then, just three days later, Jesus called my name again.

I had stayed up all night. Watching for the first sign of the sun rising over the hills. I couldn't wait. Even before the sun rose over the hills, I ran—straight to his grave, ready to anoint his body and prepare it for eternal rest.

As I ran along the road, I wondered how I'd roll away the boulder at the entrance of the tomb. Surely a gardener—or a guard—would be there to help.

But all I saw was a black hole in the mountain. The entrance to the cave wasn't blocked by a stone after all. I sank to my knees and peered through the hole. Empty! Jesus was gone! The clothes he'd been wrapped in lay on the ground.

I gasped and looked around. *Who took Jesus?*

I got up, lifted my skirts, and ran as fast as I could back to Simon Peter and John. I told them Jesus had been stolen, but they didn't believe me. (I was a woman, after all. Just because Jesus trusted me didn't mean they would.)

So they ran themselves. John pushed Simon out of the way to make sure he got there first.

Only when they saw the empty tomb for themselves did they believe me. But they left again nearly as soon as they'd gotten there. They had run from the cross, and now they ran from the tomb.

But I couldn't leave. *My Jesus! Gone!* I fell to my knees in front of his tomb and sobbed. As I wiped my nose on my arm, a light caught my eye. A light inside the tomb! I looked in and saw two figures sitting where Jesus had been.

"Woman," they said, "why are you crying?"

I gasped. Who were they? I leaned in closer. They looked like angels. Like the ones Jesus' mother had told us about.

So I answered them: "They have taken my Lord away. I don't know where they put him."

Just then I heard something move in the gravel behind me. I turned slowly, expecting to see a guard with his sword drawn.

Instead, I faced a gardener. I jumped at the sight of him.

"Woman, why are you crying?" he said. I blinked at him. Could no one understand why I would cry for

Fast Facts

◊ Mary Magdalene is mentioned in the Gospels more than most of the apostles.

◊ Mary is thought to be from Magdala, a town on the Sea of Galilee.

◊ Mary was a key witness at Jesus' crucifixion, his empty tomb, and his resurrection.

◊ Since she was the first to share the good news of Jesus' resurrection, she is often called "The Apostle to the Apostles."

◊ It's remarkable that Jesus chose her to testify to his resurrection. Women in those days weren't considered reliable. But Jesus thought differently!

Get the Full Story
John 20:1-18

my lost Jesus?

Then the man added, "Who are you looking for?"

Voices raged once again in my head. Voices of panic. Of despair. Voices telling me all was lost, now that Jesus was gone. Voices telling me that without Jesus, I'd go back to who I'd been. To the mess I was. Frantic, I grabbed the gardener's arm.

"Please, sir, if you've taken him away, tell me where he is and I will get him."

And then I heard it. The kindness. The love. The joy. The peace. All spoken in one word: my name.

"Mary," the man said.

Mary.

And the voices in my head went silent.

The world around me faded away. Rocks and bushes blurred into the background. The sky grew strangely dim. But the man in front of me grew brighter and clearer and sharper before my eyes.

Jesus.

I gasped. My knees buckled. It was Jesus!

Jesus smiled and reached his arm to steady me.

"*Robboni,*" I said as I wrapped my own arms around him.

Jesus. My teacher. My friend. The one who stilled the

voices. The one who saved me. The one who loved me. He was here. He was alive. He had risen from the dead!

I stepped back to look at him. To make sure it was really Jesus. It was. Scars lined his forehead. Deep circles marked his hands. My Jesus! I leaned back into him and hugged him tight. I never wanted to let go.

But then, Jesus backed away. He held my hands and took a deep breath.

"You can't hold on to me forever," Jesus said. "I must return to my Father—and yours. To my God—and your God. But I need you to go tell my brothers what you've seen."

I'll never know what compelled me to leave. Where I found the strength to tear myself away from the One who had quieted the voices and who had loved me like no other. But I did as Jesus asked. I held my sandals in my hand as I ran back to find Simon Peter and John again, to find Andrew and James, to find Matthew and Mark.

"I have seen the Lord!" I told them.

They didn't believe me. But they'd learn soon enough. They'd be puzzled about why Jesus had chosen a woman to see him first. They'd be puzzled about why he'd chosen *me* to share the good news before anyone else.

To be honest, I was just as puzzled. That Jesus chose me: the woman once controlled by voices in her head.

But then, I hear Jesus calling my name: *Mary*. And I have a guess. Jesus showed me the power of what speaking a name in love can do, how it can drive off "demons" and save a life.

I've spent the rest of my life sharing that same thing. Not my name, of course. Silly Mary. No, it's *this* name I say now: *Jesus*. Only Jesus.

Think About It

Think about the different ways people say your name. What makes each different? Special?

What negative thoughts about yourself do you struggle to ignore?

What messages does Jesus give you that could overpower those negative thoughts?

Prayer Prompt

Find somewhere quiet to sit. Maybe your room. Maybe a closet. Sit down and close your eyes. Breathe in and breathe out. Thank God for calling you by name. Ask Jesus to help you focus on the love he has for you. And ask him to help you ignore those negative thoughts that sometimes overwhelm our minds. Ask God to remind you how wonderful and loved you are.

Chapter 13

The Samaritan Woman

"**N**o, no, no!"

The donkey ignored me and continued to lap up the water that spilled around her feet.

I should've known better than to let Jonas tie her to the porch for the night. Last time she was there, she ate through the rug I'd patched up for the woman down the street—ruined

Age: Unknown

Era: 32 CE

the little bit of work I'd managed to take in recently. And now? She'd kicked over our water for the day.

I had no choice. I'd have to go back to the well.

The hot sun beat down on me. But I was used to it by now. This wouldn't be my first trip to Jacob's Well in the middle of the day. Sure, I'd have to push my way through crowds in the marketplace (they all stopped bartering over the price of wheat and figs, pomegranates and wine to point and whisper as I walked by). But at least I'd be alone at the well. No other women around to ask me about Jonas, to mention that they had seen his donkey out front again, and to wonder if he would ever propose marriage.

There'd be no women like the nosy Rebekah, who just last week asked if I was being good to Jonas or if I'd "run this one off too" with my "high and mighty questions."

"Women have no business bothering men with such things!" Rebekah had said.

What did Rebekah know? She just believed everything anyone told her. She never questioned. She never wondered. Sure, she still had a husband, but what kind of life did they have? Just Rebekah smiling and nodding as he rambled on? What kind of marriage is that?

No, thank you. I wasn't going to stop wanting to know why we worshipped the way we did. Why God only answered our prayers sometimes. And why the Jews hated us so, when we shared Jacob—the one who built the well—as an ancestor.

People said I drove my husbands to an early grave—or just plain away—with my questions.

Maybe they were right. But surely, there had to be a man who would welcome my questions.

I slowed my steps as I approached the well. A man sat on the edge. His head rested in his hands. A satchel lay at his feet. A traveler. An exhausted one at that. Probably harmless—but still, strange men made me nervous.

So I looked around, hoping to see someone—anyone—else within earshot. Just in case this wasn't a kind stranger. No matter, I realized. He'd get up and run as soon as he realized he was alone with a woman. Especially a woman like me.

As I set down my jar, the man lifted his head. And then he smiled.

Our eyes met for a moment before I looked away, ashamed. His face, browned and wrinkled from the sun, looked like he'd traveled a long way. But his eyes, soft and kind, looked like they could see into my soul.

"Excuse me," the man said. "Could I trouble you for some water?"

I stepped back.

A Jew! I could hear it in his voice. Now that I looked closer, I could see it in the style of his bag.

My eyes widened. Could I have heard him correctly? No self-respecting Jewish man would ever ask me, a Samaritan woman, for a drink. Whatever I touched was unclean for them. I should have disgusted him.

"Sir," I said, "you know you're in Samaria, right? And you must know I'm Samaritan. How can you ask me for water?"

The man laughed. But it wasn't a mean laugh. He wasn't making fun of my silly question. He laughed like he was glad I asked. Like he *liked* my question.

"Ma'am," he said, "if you knew who was asking you for water, you'd ask *me* for some of my living water."

Fast Facts

◊ **This is the first time Jesus told anyone he was the Messiah. For generations, the Jewish people had believed in God's promise that one day they would have a Savior, a Messiah. It's pretty cool that it was a woman who recognized Jesus for who he was.**

◊ **The Samaritan Woman was remarkable both for being the first woman preacher (more would come soon!) and for engaging in discussion with Jesus about spiritual things. Women weren't usually included in those kinds of conversations back then.**

◊ **The Jewish people and the Samaritans had a long history of mutual suspicion and animosity, which sometimes turned violent. It was a big deal for Jesus to talk to anyone from Samaria, let alone a woman.**

Now *I* laughed. It came out meaner than I wanted. I corrected myself with a small courtesy.

"Well, sir, just how would you get this 'living water'?" I said. "You don't even have anything to draw it. Are you mightier than our ancestor Jacob, who used this well for his family and his animals?"

He just smiled at me again. I shook my head and lowered the pail into the well. I drew it up slowly and handed it to the man. I sat next to him as he gulped at the water, not minding at all that it was a Samaritan who had given it to him.

Get the Full Story
John 4:1-42

I raised my eyebrows and tapped my fingers. I was waiting for my answer. The man wiped the drops that had spilled on his chin, took a breath, and thanked me.

"But you know," he said, "I'll be thirsty again. So will you. In fact, anyone who drinks this water will be thirsty again. But the living water I offer becomes a bubbling spring forever. You'll never be thirsty again."

I stared at him for a second. Was this guy for real? I didn't know. But I decided to bite. I'd see where this rabbit trail led.

"Okay," I said. "I'm sick of coming to this well. I'm sick of the gossips who hang out here and tease me. Give me some of this water so I don't have to come here anymore."

The man smiled. I was beginning to enjoy his smile.

I'd never seen anything like it.

"All right," he said. "Just go get your husband and you got it."

Ugh. Him too?

I looked him right in the eyes and said, "I don't have a husband."

"I know. But you have had five. And the man you live with now isn't your husband."

I searched his face, looked into the deep wrinkles, the bright eyes, searching for any sign of anger or cruelty, but I didn't see any. Only kindness. His words weren't mean— but they were true. Like he just wanted me to know that he saw me, that he knew me, that he understood.

Suddenly, I understood too.

"Sir," I said, "you're a prophet."

The man nodded.

"So, can you answer a question for me?"

He nodded. "Happily."

"Our ancestors worshipped God right on this mountain. But now the Jews say the only place we can worship God is in Jerusalem. Why is that? Are they right?"

"Good questions," the man said. "But here's the thing: Soon, you won't worship God on this mountain *or* in Jerusalem. A time is coming when we'll worship God 'in spirit and in truth.' Those are the kind of worshippers God wants—people who seek God everywhere. Because

God is Spirit—and is everywhere—God wants people to worship not just in one place but with all their hearts, their souls, and their minds."

My mind spun. I had a million questions. But this is what came out of my mouth (I have no idea why): "I can't wait for the Messiah, the Christ, to come. He'll explain all this to me."

"Well, he's *trying* to explain all this to you," the man said, with a laugh. "I am the Messiah."

I slid off the side of the wall, instinctively knelt at his feet.

Just then, a small group of men approached—his friends, returning from town.

"Jesus?" one of them asked. Of course, they were shocked to find him with me. But no one was more shocked than I. The Messiah! I had so many questions. But first, I had to tell someone. Jonas! Rebekah! The people at market! They needed to know! The Messiah! He was here! And he *came* here! To *us!* The Samaritans!

I hugged Jesus' feet and got up to run to town. I left my unfilled jar at the well. But it didn't matter. I had living water.

Jesus stayed in our town for two more days. His friends weren't thrilled about bunking up with a bunch of Samaritans and eating our "unclean" food. And they didn't seem to love all the questions I asked.

But Jesus did. He answered them—sometimes with other questions. Which I liked. It was like he trusted me to do my own thinking.

I became a preacher that day at the well. And from then on, nobody cared how many husbands I'd had. They wanted to know what it was like to sit with the Messiah, to have him smile at me and drink from my cup.

It was life changing. I still can't fully explain it. But I usually start with: "The Messiah is the one man who welcomed me, my messy life, and my big questions."

Think About It

Jesus doesn't seem concerned about talking to a woman he should have seen as "unclean." What does that tell you about Jesus?

Why do you think Jesus seems to enjoy the Samaritan Woman's questions?

Imagine you just bumped into Jesus one day. What questions would you ask him?

Prayer Prompt

Asking questions is one of the best ways to grow in our faith. Pray for the courage to wonder out loud and stay curious about your faith.

Chapter 14

The Bleeding Woman

Years.

Every day.

For years.

~~~~~~~~~~~~~~~~~~~~~~~~~~~~~~~~~~~~~

Age: Unknown. But she'd had her period for 12 years straight, so she was either in her early 20s or in her 60s.

Era: 30–33 CE

~~~~~~~~~~~~~~~~~~~~~~~~~~~~~~~~~~~~~

That's how long I've been bleeding.

I bleed because I'm not pregnant.

It's what women do. When there's no baby in the womb, the body sheds what we had to nourish a baby.

But I have no babies. In fact, no babies will ever grow in my body.

Instead, blood does. It comes out not just for a short time each month, but constantly.

All day.

Nonstop.

Every day. For years.

The doctors have tried to help me. But they can't.

It's awful.

I'm tired.

I'm crabby.

But the worst part is, I'm so lonely.

Being a good Jewish woman means as long as I bleed, I'm unclean.

Dirty.

I'm not welcome around others. Whatever I touch, whomever I touch, becomes dirty too.

So all day I stay alone.

I want to die. . . .

But then one day I hear news: Jesus is coming to my town.

Jesus, the one who gives sight to the blind and clean skin to the lepers.

Jesus is here.

He can heal me. He can make the bleeding stop.

Jesus can make me clean.

So I get up. Even though all the blood I lose makes me dizzy when I stand. Even though the blood runs down my legs and stains my robes.

I pull my scarf tighter over my head and head out my door.

First, I follow the sounds of the crowds. Then I press my way through them.

When others see the blood, they scream and shuffle away.

I should turn back. I'm disobeying the Law. But I keep going. I push and shove and make everyone around me unclean.

Until I reach Jesus. Or almost reach him. Because he's there, just a few people ahead of me.

But I know: even one touch, even one little

Get the Full Story
Mark 5:21-34, Luke 8:40-48

Fast Facts

◊ **When a Jewish woman in Jesus' time had her period, she was considered "unclean" for seven days from the start of her period. If anyone touched her or sat on something she had sat on, they were unclean for the rest of the day. These laws were based on the ancient Jewish laws listed in the Old Testament book of Leviticus.**

◊ **Some people believe this woman followed Jesus to the cross and wiped his forehead as he was dying.**

◊ **Jesus healed this woman on his way to heal a synagogue leader's dead daughter.**

brush against him, will make me clean.

I stretch my hand through the crowd and grab the tassel of his robe. He doesn't even know I'm there.

Something surges through my body. My womb tenses for a second, and then all is still. I've been healed. I feel it. I know it.

Jesus turns around. As though something has surged through him too.

I've been caught. I've just touched a rabbi.

A holy man. I knew I was unclean, but I touched him anyway.

I cower. Terrified.

"Who touched me?" Jesus asks.

The crowd backs away. They point at me. Someone snickers. Another scoffs. I start to cry.

I step forward. I fall at Jesus' feet and tell him everything. About the blood. About the dizziness. About the loneliness.

I can't stop shaking.

Jesus kneels down and lays his hand on my back.

The crowd gasps.

I freeze.

No one has touched me in 12 years.

"Daughter," Jesus says, "your faith has healed you. Go in peace and be freed from your suffering."

Jesus touched me.

Jesus touched me!

Jesus touched me and made me clean.

Jesus touched me and made me worthy.

Jesus touched me and set me free.

Think About It

The law that kept the Bleeding Woman so lonely seems so unfair. How do you respond when you have to follow rules that don't make sense or that seem unfair?

Other people backed away from this "dirty" woman, but Jesus approached her. What does that tell you about Jesus? What does that tell you about how Jesus might want us to treat others?

Jesus says that the woman's faith healed her. What do you think she had faith in?

Prayer Prompt

What's a big step of faith you could take? As you pray, ask God to help you develop the courage you need to take big risks in your faith.

Chapter 15

Dorcas

The voices around me drifted and dulled. Soon, I couldn't hear anything more than a faint din—the way you hear a party at a faraway neighbor's, or someone singing in the distance.

I couldn't make out words or phrases or even figure out if they were voices for sure. But there was something.

Something that kept me connected. Like I wasn't fully gone.

And yet, I *was* dead. I knew that. If I would've opened my eyes in this new place, I would've been surrounded by light. A light that fired up all your senses. Because I could *feel* it. I could almost smell it. I knew it was there—even with my eyes closed. I could feel a warming all around me, a brightening, the kind you sense as the sun rises outside your window.

That's what my first few moments of death were like. But there was something else: there was a peace, a calmness, a state of being relaxed, like I'd never known.

I suppose it could've been because my life had not included anything close to relaxation. I'd been a busy woman. Always. I'd worked hard, creating some of the finest fashions in Joppa, the town where I'm from.

Age: Unknown. Most likely middle-age or older since she was probably a widow and a woman with some money to her name.

Era: First century

I'd sketch out patterns for robes and dresses, light coats and shawls, and present the sketches, along with the finest fabric samples, to the town's richest women. They'd placed orders for my creations long before I took needle and thread to linen or silk. Everyone wanted my clothes. I made a good living for myself and provided a good life to my family.

But something changed one day a few years ago. A couple of missionaries came to Joppa and told us about a man named Jesus. Jesus had died—and risen again! As if that weren't enough to intrigue me, these missionaries told of what Jesus had preached. Things like the fact that we could be forgiven—guilt-free—for bad things we'd done. I'd never heard this before. I thought living with guilt was just part of life. And I figured what happened to us in death was up to God—or the gods, as my Greek friends believed.

Fast Facts

◊ Because Dorcas lived in an area with both Jewish and Greek people, Luke (who wrote her story) uses both her Jewish name (Tabitha) and her Greek name (Dorcas). Both names mean "gazelle": the beautiful, fast, and strong deer-like animal.

◊ Dorcas was called a disciple.

◊ Even though she was Jewish, Dorcas would have adopted much of the Greek life and language around her.

There was more. This Jesus spoke of the ways we were to love one another. We should love others—our best neighbors and our worst enemies—as we loved *ourselves*. I took that to mean we were to *care* for others the way we cared for ourselves. So I thought of how my children and I dressed—beautifully. I thought of how my children and I ate—till we were full. And I thought of how others dressed—in old, tattered clothes. And I thought of how others ate—whatever they could scavenge.

And something just clicked—in my heart, mind, and soul.

I wanted not only to know more about this Jesus; I wanted to live as he lived. I'd always been a hard worker— but I'd worked hard for myself. Now I wanted to work hard for others.

So I did that. I kept making clothes for the rich and powerful, but I also made clothes for the poor and overlooked. What the rich could pay for their clothes made up for what the poor could not.

Where once I'd felt great pride in seeing the rich women of my town wearing my fashions, now I took greater pride in seeing the women who begged in alleys and women who worked endless hours at mills and wine presses dressed in my best designs. And the children! If I may say so, the kids of our town never looked better. Kids who'd never known a new robe and had grown used to patching hole after hole after hole now wore clothes that would last them for years.

Using my skills to help others was a joy I'd never known. Living for Jesus changed my life.

But then one day, the headaches set in. I could no longer focus on the needle and thread. I could no longer tell one color from another, as I could no longer tolerate being in the light.

I thought the headaches would pass. That just a day or two in bed with a cold cloth on my forehead would help. I heard my servants turning away women and children at the door. I could hear their cries as my maid said, "Miss Dorcas is not well. She has no clothes for you today."

I tried to get up, to tell the women to come back

tomorrow, but I was too weak. I couldn't even speak.

Get the Full Story

Acts 9:36-43

And then the voices around me dulled. Grew distant. Until I couldn't hear them anymore. Until I landed here. In death.

I was dead. If I opened my eyes, I'd see this light I felt around me. I'd see Jesus. I knew it. I wanted to. Until I heard something else.

Not yet, Dorcas. Not yet.

It was just as I had imagined Jesus' voice whenever people told me the stories of his life. So welcoming. So comforting. So true. So right.

Not yet. Not yet, Jesus had said.

So I didn't open my eyes. Not yet. I just enjoyed the peace. Enjoyed being free of the headache, finally.

Until I heard another voice. One I'd never heard before.

The voice called me by my *real* name: Tabitha.

"Tabitha," the voice said, "get up."

And so I did.

I opened my eyes and saw a man. I sat up and asked who he was.

"I'm Peter," he said. And he took my hand and helped me stand.

Peter. I knew that name from the stories of Jesus. Peter

was the Rock, on whom Jesus said he'd build his church. But building churches only reminded me: I had work to do.

So I thanked Peter but said, "If you'll excuse me, I have clothes to make."

Peter laughed, praised God, and called out that I was alive.

Soon everyone in town was back at my house, crying and celebrating. Peter told more stories of Jesus' healing powers, and many more people believed that day.

And I just kept making clothes.

Think About It

How do you feel about stories of people who have "come back to life"? Do you believe them? Why or why not?

Dorcas spent her days doing good deeds for others. How could you use a talent or interest you already have to do good things for other people?

Prayer Prompt

Talk with God about ways you can help other people. Pay attention to the opportunities God puts in front of you to show kindness, generosity, and compassion.

Chapter 16

The One-Hit Wonders

I'm Lydia.

I'm Phoebe.

I'm Priscilla.

We are the One-Line Wonders.

Of course, no one ever called us that. Because it's not even right—even though it sounds good.

We each get little mentions in Luke's accounts of the early church and in Paul's letters, but Bible readers don't know much else about us, other than our names, where we're from, and a bit of what we did. You don't get our full stories—or even *a* full story.

So maybe you know that Lydia sold fancy purple cloth, listened to Paul, and opened her heart to Jesus.

And maybe you know Phoebe was a deacon and a leader.

Priscilla gets a shout-out from Paul for her missionary work, her teaching, her hospitality, and her wild sense of adventure (Priscilla got around!).

But really, the Bible doesn't say much about us beyond a sentence or two. We're mysteries!

And yet, even though we laugh about our minimal mentions, truth is: We represent thousands of other women whose names we'll never know but who shaped human history. Who lived out the great stories of the Bible, the great work of the love story of God and God's people. Who listened at Jesus' feet, followed him, and preached his good news.

Ages of these women: Unknown, although they all had households of their own, so they were at least 20.

Era: First century

It can be easy to forget how front-and-center women are to the story of God.

Dorothy Sayers, a writer who lived thousands of years after us, wrote this:

> Perhaps it is no wonder that the women were first at the Cradle and last at the Cross. They had never known a man like this Man—there never has been such another. A prophet and teacher who never nagged at them, never flattered or coaxed or patronized; who never made arch jokes about them, never treated them either as "The women, God help us!" or "The ladies, God bless them!"; who rebuked without querulousness and praised without condescension; who took their questions and arguments seriously; who never mapped out their sphere for them, never urged them to be feminine or jeered at them for being female; who had no axe to grind and no uneasy male dignity to defend; who took them as he found them and was completely unself-conscious. There is no act, no sermon, no parable in the whole Gospel that borrows its pungency from female perversity; nobody could possibly guess from the words and deeds of Jesus that there was anything "funny" about woman's nature.

In other words: Jesus treated every woman he met with love, care, and kindness. Even when society taught that he shouldn't, he touched and listened to and healed women who had been forgotten and ignored and ridiculed. He changed our lives. And that's why we told his story everywhere we went.

Yes, we still lived with some weird rules about who we could talk to and where we could go and what we could do. And yes, sometimes the stories in the Bible make it seem as though men got to do everything important. But our stories—and the stories of other women like us—make it clear that was never true.

Here's what is true:

God has always paid attention to the pain and fear and longing of women.

Women have always been essential in the story of God.

Women—and girls like you—matter to God and have important work to do

Fast Facts

Lydia:

◊ She was probably wealthy and had high social standing, although some think she may have once been a slave.

◊ She was a founding member of a house church. Though a woman leading a religious ceremony would've shocked Jewish people, in Lydia's Greek culture, it wasn't unusual.

Phoebe:

◊ Paul calls her a deacon and a patron, which means a financial supporter of the church.

◊ Her name means "bright one."

Priscilla:

◊ Her name is listed before her husband's in the Bible. This is significant and may mean she had a higher social standing than he did— or that she was more active in the church than he was.

◊ She and her husband were tent makers, which means they did other jobs to make money to support their missionary work.

◊ Priscilla actually shows up in eight different passages. Paul greets her in three different letters, which is how we know she traveled!

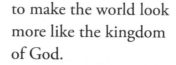

Get the Full Story

Acts 16:14 and Romans 16:1-5

to make the world look more like the kingdom of God.

And whether you ever get a mention in a book about how you live for Jesus doesn't matter. It's just about how you live and how you love.

But living and loving take courage. They always have and always will.

It wasn't easy for any of us to listen to God or follow in the way of Jesus. It didn't fit what our families or cultures expected from us.

But God gave us a path that's always worth following.

Think About It

What are some things you can do today that your mom or aunts or grandmothers couldn't do when they were your age?

How does it change your sense of yourself to know that God has plans for you?

What do you wish other girls your age knew about Jesus?

Prayer Prompt

Ask God to keep you filled up with a belief that you are created in the image of God and made to do big things in God's name. Really. You are.

Acknowledgments

People like to ask writers where we get our ideas. I've heard some writers act like it's some big mystery or unexplainable event. Not so. Ideas are all around us. If you want to write and need an idea: pay attention to the world and sometimes stop to wonder, "What if . . . " Then, start writing. Easy.

Which is why I need to start by thanking Cynthia Dermody and Natalie van der Mere for assigning me a story about beautiful baby girl names from the Bible. After spending a morning looking up names and reading the stories behind them, I had the good sense to ask a few different, "What if . . . ?" questions, and an idea was born.

But ideas are the easy part. Which is why I need to thank the many people who helped with this project along the way. Thanks to:

Carla Barnhill, for your listening ear, your brainstorms, and of course, for championing it—and guiding it to publication.

Rachel Klooster, for your mad research and organizational skills

Naomi Krueger, for your shaping and steering skills.

Katy Betz, for your beautiful illustrations.

Marc Olson, for keeping me orthodox.

Heather Flies, for your helpful insights.

Heidi Mann, for your eagle eyes.

And for everyone at Sparkhouse Family for believing in this book.

My writers groups: The Okay Jesus Fan Club and Ink Creative Collective. The grit and grace shown among all of you inspires me every day.

My family. Thank you Mom and Dad for not only taking me to church and raising me to know God and know he made me for big things, but also for buying me those little books (and all the big books too). Thank you to my husband, Rafael, and my kids, Henrik, Greta, and Fredrik for loving me despite my writerly habits that often interfere with life. And thank you to my pit bull, Sierra, for keeping me company while I write. And for letting me know when a storm's rolling in. Love you all.